CAMBRIDGE LIBRARY COLLECTION

Books of enduring scholarly value

Cambridge

The city of Cambridge received its royal charter in 1201, having already been home to Britons, Romans and Anglo-Saxons for many centuries. Cambridge University was founded soon afterwards and celebrates its octocentenary in 2009. This series explores the history and influence of Cambridge as a centre of science, learning, and discovery, its contributions to national and global politics and culture, and its inevitable controversies and scandals.

The Cambridge Medical School

In the original statutes of the University of Cambridge, the Faculties of Physic, Theology and Law had the same formal status. The development of the teaching of medicine at Cambridge over the next 700 years was, however, neither rapid nor smooth. The first recorded medical degrees were awarded in the 1460s; a Professorship of Physic was finally endowed in 1540 by Henry VIII. Sadly, early holders of this Regius Chair generally gave priority to the pursuit of their own interests over the burden of educating medical students. It was the 1817 appointment of Dr John Haviland that ushered in the modern era of medical education and research at Cambridge. This history, first published in 1932, describes the stages in this process, focusing on the individuals who were key to its success and who laid the foundations for the respected clinical school and leading medical research laboratories of Cambridge today.

Cambridge University Press has long been a pioneer in the reissuing of out-of-print titles from its own backlist, producing digital reprints of books that are still sought after by scholars and students but could not be reprinted economically using traditional technology. The Cambridge Library Collection extends this activity to a wider range of books which are still of importance to researchers and professionals, either for the source material they contain, or as landmarks in the history of their academic discipline.

Drawing from the world-renowned collections in the Cambridge University Library, and guided by the advice of experts in each subject area, Cambridge University Press is using state-of-the-art scanning machines in its own Printing House to capture the content of each book selected for inclusion. The files are processed to give a consistently clear, crisp image, and the books finished to the high quality standard for which the Press is recognised around the world. The latest print-on-demand technology ensures that the books will remain available indefinitely, and that orders for single or multiple copies can quickly be supplied.

The Cambridge Library Collection will bring back to life books of enduring scholarly value across a wide range of disciplines in the humanities and social sciences and in science and technology.

The Cambridge Medical School

A Biographical History

Humphrey Davy Rolleston

CAMBRIDGE
UNIVERSITY PRESS

CAMBRIDGE UNIVERSITY PRESS

Cambridge New York Melbourne Madrid Cape Town Singapore São Paolo Delhi

Published in the United States of America by Cambridge University Press, New York

www.cambridge.org
Information on this title: www.cambridge.org/9781108003438

© in this compilation Cambridge University Press 2009

This edition first published 1932
This digitally printed version 2009

ISBN 978-1-108-00343-8

THE
CAMBRIDGE MEDICAL SCHOOL

LONDON
Cambridge University Press
FETTER LANE

NEW YORK · TORONTO
BOMBAY · CALCUTTA · MADRAS
Macmillan

TOKYO
Maruzen Company Ltd

IOHANNES CAIUS M.D.
(From the Picture in the College Hall)

THE
CAMBRIDGE MEDICAL SCHOOL

A Biographical History

BY

SIR HUMPHRY DAVY ROLLESTON, *Bart.*
G.C.V.O., K.C.B., M.D., Hon. D.Sc.
D.C.L., LL.D.

*Regius Professor of Physic in the University
of Cambridge; Physician-in-Ordinary to
H.M. The King; sometime President
of the Royal College of Physicians
of London*

CAMBRIDGE
AT THE UNIVERSITY PRESS
1932

CONTENTS

List of Plates . . . . . *page* vii

Preface ix

I.   The Medical School 1

II.   Department of Anatomy . . . 47

III.   Department of Physiology . . . 79

IV.   Department of Biochemistry . . . 98

V.   Department of Experimental Psychology . 100

VI.   Department of Pathology . . . 102

VII.   Department of the Quick Chair of Biology 117

VIII.   The Regius Chair of Physic . . . 120

IX.   John Caius 190

X.   The Downing Chair of Medicine . . 199

XI.   The Linacre Lectureship in Physic . . 213

XII.   The Chair of Surgery 221

Index of Persons 225

Index of Subjects 231

PLATES

John Caius, M.D., P.R.C.P.   *frontispiece*
From a portrait in the hall of Gonville and Caius College

William Heberden the Elder, M.D., F.R.S. *facing page* 18
From an engraving by James Ward of the portrait by
Sir W. Beechey, R.A.

Professor Sir George Murray Humphry, M.D.,
F.R.S.   73

Professor Alexander Macalister, M.D., F.R.S.   77

Professor Sir Michael Foster, K.C.B., M.D.,
F.R.S.   89
Photograph by the late R. A. Bickersteth, M.B., F.R.C.S.

Professor J. N. Langley, Sc.D., F.R.S.   93

W. H. Gaskell, M.D., F.R.S.   95

Professor C. S. Roy, M.D., F.R.S.   109

Professor A. A. Kanthack, M.D., F.R.C.P.,
F.R.C.S.   111

Professor Sir German Sims Woodhead, K.B.E.,
M.D.   115
Photograph by Palmer Clark, Cambridge

Robert Glynn Clobery, M.D.   122
From an engraving by I. G. and G. S. Facius of the portrait
by Thomas Kerrich

Donation-Bookplate   146
For Professor John Collins's books left to St John's College

Professor Francis Glisson, M.D., F.R.S., P.R.C.P.   153
From an engraving by W. Faithorne of his portrait of Glisson

Professor Robert Brady, M.D., F.R.C.P. *facing page* 156
From a print by Edward Harding; by courtesy of the Wellcome
Historical Medical Museum

Professor Sir Isaac Pennington, M.D., F.R.C.P.   165
From Ackermann's *History of the University of Cambridge*

Professor John Haviland, M.D., F.R.C.P.   168
From a drawing by Wageman; by courtesy of H. A. Haviland,
M.B.

Professor H. J. H. Bond, M.D., F.R.C.P.   172

Professor Sir George Paget, K.C.B., M.D.,
F.R.S.   178
Photograph by the late A. G. Dew-Smith, M.A.

Professor Right Hon. Sir Clifford Allbutt, K.C.B.,
M.D., F.R.S.   184

Professor Sir Busick Harwood, M.D., F.R.S.   201
From an engraving by W. N. Gardiner of a water-colour by
S. Harding; by courtesy of the British Museum

Sir Thomas Watson, Bart., M.D., F.R.S.,
P.R.C.P.   216
From an engraving by F. Holl, after George Richmond, R.A.

PREFACE

Acknowledgments to works of reference and authorities have been made in the text. But in addition, and without thus seeking shelter for doubtless many shortcomings, I am much indebted for help of various kinds to Professors P. H. Winfield, H. R. Dean, J. Barcroft, and A. C. Seward, Drs J. A. Venn and W. H. L. Duckworth, Lady Thomson, R. E. Priestley, First Assistant-Registrary of the University of Cambridge, and L. W. G. Malcolm, Conservator of the Wellcome Historical Medical Museum. For great assistance with the indexes I would express my gratitude to Horace M. Barlow, Bedell and Secretary, Royal College of Physicians of London.

H. D. R.

I. *The Medical School of Cambridge*

THE history of the Medical School presents two distinct phases—a long period of somnolence, like that of the new-born infant, followed in the nineteenth century and after by the stage of progressive growth and activity. From the earliest days of the University until the last quarter of the nineteenth century the number of medical students in residence was small, and until the early nineteenth century those responsible for the Faculty of Medicine, which had existed from the first, were much inclined to treat their posts as sinecures.

As far back as the end of the twelfth century Cambridge was probably a place of study where schools of "glomery" or grammar existed. But "the earliest authentic instrument" containing any recognition of Cambridge as a University is a writ of the second year (February 17, 1217–18) of Henry III,[1] a century before it received formal

1 Peacock (*Observations on the Statutes of the University of Cambridge*, p. 14, 1841), however, gives 1231 as the earliest public and official recognition of the University of Cambridge as an organized body of Masters and scholars by Henry III. According to Hastings Rashdall (*The Universities of Europe in the Middle Ages*, vol. II, part 2, p. 543, 1895), the earliest date at which Cambridge can be regarded as a *Studium generale* is 1209, when the Masters and scholars at Oxford hastily migrated on account of disturbances there, some of them coming to Cambridge, which thus owes its *Studium generale* to this *Suspendium Clericorum* of 1209. As no evidence is brought forward that this was the starting-point of student life at Cambridge, Gray (*Cambridge University: An*

recognition as a *Studium generale respectu regni* or *Universitas* by a Bull from Pope John XXII in 1318. The Collegiate system was inaugurated in 1284 by Hugh de Balsham (*obiit* 1286), tenth Bishop of Ely, who founded Peterhouse (Domus Scholarium Sancti Petri) twenty years after Merton College, Oxford, was established by Walter de Merton (*obiit* 1277), Lord Chancellor.

The statutes of the University, like those of Oxford, were closely modelled on those of Paris which was a "Master-University", or Corporation of Masters or teachers, in contradistinction to the "Student-Universities", such as Bologna and Padua, in which the students' guilds largely chose and controlled the teachers. The original statutes of Cambridge placed the Faculty of Physic on the same footing as those of Theology and Law, and, though the records about medical instruction before 1500 are scanty, the provisions for teaching and graduating in these three faculties were on the same lines. As in Italian Universities of the Middle Ages, there were three grades in Medicine, Doctor, Baccalaureus, and Practicantes (in Medicine [M.L.] and in Chirurgie [C.L.]). The earliest existing Grace Book shows that the first recorded degree of M.D. was that conferred on James Fries or Freis in 1460–1, and that one Lemster in 1466–7

Episodical History, 1926) suggests that the Oxonians came to Cambridge because teaching was then known to be going on there. At Oxford the real beginning of a *Studium generale* was in or about 1167. The mythical existence of Cambridge as a town and University at much earlier dates is mentioned in the sketch of John Caius (p. 196).

was the first to receive the degree of M.B.[1] That the Universities had "Scoles of Fisyk" with a recognized reputation early in the fifteenth century appears to be borne out by the presentation on May 2, 1421, of the petition to Parliament praying that the practice of physic should be restricted to those who had graduated in that faculty at the Universities or had been approved by these bodies. This request was granted, and it was also enacted that no woman should practise physic and that the penalty for so doing would be a fine to be paid to the King and a long term of imprisonment.

According to the *Statuta antiqua* (*vide* p. 45) candidates for the M.D. degree must have acted as regents in Arts, namely have taken the M.A. degree, and then have attended lectures for five years at Cambridge or some other University, making twelve years in all, two of which must have been spent in the practice of medicine. This last clause about clinical experience, probably taken from the regulations of Montpellier, was the first enactment in this country necessitating practical acquaintance with medical work. Otherwise the provisions with regard to time, form, and subjects were bookish and almost the same as those of the medical faculty of Paris in 1272. The textbooks and courses set out in the Old Proctors' Book about

[1] The degree of Doctor of Medicine was first conferred in this country in 1449–50 by the University of Oxford on Thomas Edmonds, where before that date the title Master of Physic was used. The B.M. degree at Oxford was first conferred in 1455 (October 19) on Thomas Bloxham, M.A. (*Register of the University of Oxford*, vol. I, 1449–1463; 1505–1571, edited by C. W. Boase, 1885). Glasgow in 1470 was the first Scottish University to confer the degree of M.D.

1396 were as follows: attendance once on the reading of the *Isagoge* of Johanitius (809–73), the *De Urinis* and *De Pulsibus* of Theophilus Protospatharius (πρωτο-σπαθάριος = colonel of the spatharii or guards), chief physician at the Byzantine Court of the Emperor Heraclius (603–41), the second of these texts appearing under the pseudonym of Philaretus (Macalister, 1904), and one of the works of Isaac Judaeus (855–955), namely either the *De Urinis*, *De Dietis particularibus*, *De Febribus*, or the *De Viatico*, and the *Antidotarium* of Nicolaus Salernitanus. The *Tegni* (τέχνη ἰατρική), *Prognostica*, *Aphorismi*, and *De Regimine Acutorum* of Galen with their commentaries must each be heard twice. "Cursory lectures must be read, treating of one book on theory and one on practice; the usual opponency and responsions are exacted...and finally all the masters of the faculty must depose of knowledge of the candidate's fitness." In these early times students commonly came into residence as boys of fourteen or even younger.

The Grace Books show that in the forty-two years 1500–41 there were conferred one M.D., one M.B., four licences to practise physic (M.L.), and four licences to practise surgery (C.L.). In the forty-eight years 1542–89 there was a great increase in the number: 63 M.D.s, 3 M.B.s, 41 M.L.s, and 17 C.L.s. The M.B. was of a less literary character than the M.D. and was evidently not popular then; the licence to practise physic seems to have been generally regarded as the equivalent of, and indeed the substitute for, the M.B.; the chief difference in procedure was that candidates for the M.L. did not have to keep an Act. The licence to practise physic was more academic than the surgical licence; for 25 out of the 41 M.L.s had graduated in Arts, and 12 out of these subsequently proceeded to the M.D.; whereas among the 17 C.L.s three only appear to have taken an Arts degree (J. Venn).

Thomas Linacre (1460?–1524), grammarian, humanist, priest, and scholar-physician, was much concerned about the state of English medicine which was under Arabian influence and largely practised by illiterate monks and quacks. Accordingly, with the help of Cardinal Wolsey, the Lord Chancellor, he persuaded Henry VIII to constitute the Royal College of Physicians of London on September 23, 1518, with the privilege of controlling and licensing practitioners first in and seven miles around London; four years later it was enacted that "no person except a graduate of Oxford or Cambridge, without dispensation, should be permitted to practise physic throughout England, unless he had previously obtained letters testimonial under seal of his having been examined and approved by the President and three of the Elects". The rule about practice in and seven miles around London gave rise to several legal actions on behalf of medical graduates of Oxford and Cambridge against the College of Physicians; thus in 1609–10 Thomas Bonham (*obiit* 1629?), M.D., of St John's College, Cambridge, brought an action against the College for false imprisonment for practising as a physician in London without their licence; the case was dismissed in the plaintiff's favour. In 1701 and 1716–17 the cases of Henry Levett, D.M., and Thomas West, D.M., both of Oxford, were decided in favour of the College (*vide* p. 159). In addition, being familiar with the medical activity in the Northern Italian Universities, Linacre, who was elected a fellow of All Souls in 1484, founded in 1524 two lectureships at Oxford and one at Cambridge, thus showing, in Fuller's words, "dutifully his respect to his mother, double above his aunt". The foundations were made public in the *Diploma Regium* on October 12, 1524, eight days before his death, the Oxford lectureships being entrusted to the care of trustees,[1] the Cambridge one directly to St John's College. To the Master, fellows, and scholars of that college he gave the "Belle and Lanthorne", variously described as 17 Addle Hill, or in Adlying or Adlinge Street in the Parish of St Bennet in Castle Baynard Ward, near St Paul's Cathedral, London, and £209 in gold to pay £12 a year to the lecturer, who every fourth year was to cease his "redying" for the space of half a year, receive £6 only, and while lecturer not to engage in private practice; nothing was then stated about the subjects of the lectures. The Statutes of Elizabeth in 1570 gave more precise directions: the

1 At Oxford there was very considerable delay on the part of the Linacre trustees in taking any action. In 1549 Thomas Rainold, Raynolds or Renolds, Warden of Merton (1545–1559), moved in the matter and obtained from Cuthbert Tunstall (1474–1559), Bishop of Durham and the surviving trustee of this Linacre bequest, the appropriation of the lectureships to Merton which was the College most frequented by medical students. It was not, however, until 1558 that the life appointment to the superior or "more" of the two readerships, with a stipend of £12 a year, was given to Robert Barnes or Barons who was elected a fellow of Merton in 1538 and died in 1604. In 1559 George James, elected a fellow in 1551, was appointed the first inferior or "less" Linacre reader, but resigned in the following year.

6

lecturer was to be at least a Master of Arts, well versed in the works of Aristotle, and to explain Galen's treatises *De Sanitate Tuenda* and *De Methodo Medendi* as translated by Linacre, or his *De Elementis et Simplicibus*. The Statutes of Victoria 1849 continued the office and directed the lecturer to deliver courses on food and drugs, the care of health, methods of healing, forensic medicine, or one or other of these subjects to be approved by the Master. The Cambridge bequest, which might with advantage have been made a University rather than a college (St John's) trust, was mismanaged and the stipends were regarded as nothing more than a welcome addition to the income of a fellow, who treated the appointment more or less as a sinecure. The college records do not show how the money was invested, but the property—17 Addle Hill—was sold to the Metropolitan Board of Works in 1865 for £4185. The College of Physicians flourished and London thus overshadowed the Universities in medical education and matters generally.

In 1540 Henry VIII established the Regius Professorships of Divinity, Civil Law, Physic, Hebrew, and Greek, all on the same footing, and thus should have ensured a living school of Medicine at Cambridge. But the results were most disappointing; for this several reasons may be ascribed. The influence of the College of Physicians may have played a small part in making the Universities so inactive, for in other countries the Universities were the only avenue to Medicine, as there were not any competing corporations corresponding to the College of Physicians; the London College, however, did not undertake any teaching. But the most important factors were inside

7

the University, which treated Medicine as but a part of general learning and exercised a very slight and varying control over students wishing to take medical degrees. In the seventeenth and eighteenth centuries mathematics, as the result of Isaac Newton's epoch-making work, became the predominant academic pursuit, and in the early nineteenth century classics began to share in this exclusive attitude. While cultivating the intellectual needs, the University atmosphere was conservatively hostile to those of the body. Medical students who wished to get real teaching were obliged to seek it elsewhere, as Harvey, Caius, and others did at Padua, and none of them when they came back to England founded a school at Cambridge; Glisson, the outstanding Regius Professor in the disturbed seventeenth century, though occupying the chair for forty-one years, was absent much of this time in London and elsewhere. On November 12, 1548, Edward VI issued a

Commission under the Great Seal constituting Thomas Goodrich Bishop of Ely, Nicholas Ridley Bishop of Rochester, Sir William Paget, K.G., Controller of His Household (also High Steward of the University 1554–1563), Thomas Smyth His Secretary, John Cheke His Tutor, William Meye, LL.D., Master of the Requests and Dean of St Paul's, and Thomas Wendye, M.D., His Physician, His Delegates and Commissaries,

to visit the University with wide powers.

Among their directions was to constitute a Medical College in some other fit place in the University by designing one of the Colleges for the study of medicine, and to make such of the fellows thereof as were willing to apply themselves to that study and should be deemed fit, fellows of the King's Medical College, and to transfer to other Colleges those who were unwilling or should be considered unfit for that art.

8

The Commissaries visited Cambridge and were there from May 5 to July 4, 1549, but did not take any action on the proposed Medical College. The Statutes directed that the textbooks to be read by the Regius Professor should be the works of Hippocrates and Galen.

Medical teaching, such as it was, from the birth of the University until the nineteenth century, consisted in the reading and expounding of Hippocrates, Galen, and Aretaeus, and was devoid of the experimental method in which Harvey could have led the way. The belief that academic prejudice was an important obstacle is supported by the analogy of events at Oxford, where during the middle of the seventeenth century there was for a time a remarkable group of men keenly interested in experimental science, the "Philosophicall Clubbe" (1647), composed of Robert Boyle, Richard Lower, Christopher Wren, Thomas Willis, John Wilkins, William Petty, John Wallis, Jonathan Goddard, and others. This was not so much the result of activity inside the University as due to the influence of men who collected there because of the disturbed conditions of the times; many of them were members of the University, though not Robert Boyle. After the Restoration (1660), however, many of them were in London and active in forming the Royal Society (founded by Charles II on July 15, 1662) in which Boyle's "Invisible" College and the scientific spirits mentioned above, who before moving to Oxford had met in connection with Gresham College, London, from 1645, were merged. Though the Oxford Philosophical Society continued to meet irregularly until 1690, their influence in the University evaporated and scientific research languished there. Thus Uffenbach in 1710 visiting the chemical laboratory fitted for the "Philosophicall Clubbe" found "the stoves in fair condition, but everything else in disorder and dirt".

In 1553 the total number of resident members of the University, including Masters, fellows, scholars, and pensioners of colleges, was, according to Caius, 1813; in 1622 the number of students in the University had increased to 2998.

In 1570 the Elizabethan Statutes, by superseding the *Statuta antiqua*, removed the requirement of a preliminary training in Arts and thus enabled students to start medical work directly they came into residence, after six years thus spent to be eligible for the degree of M.B., and five years later, or eleven years in all, for that of M.D. This radical change resulted in a large number of Cambridge medical graduates dispensing with a degree in Arts (*vide* p. 24), until in the last quarter of the nineteenth century the Natural Sciences Tripos, which included human anatomy, physiology, botany, comparative anatomy, and chemistry, gave the B.A. degree for proficiency in subjects forming part of the medical curriculum. The Elizabethan relaxation of the demands for a more general education in the "old humanities" has a bearing on the Statute of the Royal College of Physicians of London, then and until March 31, 1835, effective, namely that the fellowship was open only to medical graduates of Oxford and Cambridge, a restriction partly based on the assumption that these graduates received the education of a scholar-physician.

On February 12, 1674-5, the King directed the Royal College of Physicians of London not to admit into their body any candidate who had not been educated and kept the Act for the M.D. degree, or had been incorporated at the Universities of Oxford and Cambridge, thus confirming the action of the College. The Elizabethan Statutes laid it down that candidates for the M.B. must have seen two dissections and "responded" twice and "opposed" once in the disputations in the schools; in 1681, however, the candidate was excused one of the Acts. The Regius Professor's duty was to read Hippocrates and Galen four days in the week, all medical students being obliged to attend, and, if the students so desired, to perform one "anatomy" a year. For nearly three hundred years the Statutes did not undergo any essential change.

A Grace of January 24, 1624–5, enabled those who had obtained the doctorate of medicine in Universities "in partibus transmarinis" to be admitted *ad eundem gradum* or to be incorporated at Cambridge, provided that they disputed *more respondentium* in that faculty at Cambridge before admission or incorporation. In 1654 William Dell, Master of Gonville and Caius (1649–1660) and John Webster (1610–1682), in his *Academiarum Examen*, both independently brought an indictment against the teaching of science including Medicine in the University. The following figures as to graduation are given by A. Macalister: between 1570 and 1658 there were conferred 178 M.D.s, 55 M.B.s, and 157 licences to practise, of which three were stated to be surgical; in the last forty-eight of the eighty-eight years there were 129 M.D.s, 53 M.B.s, and 85 licences to practise, showing a very great increase in the numbers. "A Register of Doctors of Physic in our

Universities of Oxford and Cambridge" from 1659 to 1694 inclusive shows that of the 211 Cambridge doctors during those thirty-six years 70, or one-third, received the doctorate by Royal mandate. The frequent exercise of the Royal prerogative of granting degrees obviously tended to impair the prestige and independence of the University. In 1660 Charles II ordered the creation of 121 Doctors of Divinity and twelve Doctors of Medicine, and in the excitement and rejoicing connected with the Restoration there was perhaps a slight excuse for the "Praevaricator", among his other gibes in his Senate House speech, asking the physicians a question "Whether it is true that Homer died of the *iliaca passio*?" which was the name used by John Arderne (1306–1390?) for what would now be called intestinal obstruction. After the Revolution of 1688–9 the Crown and the University came to an agreement that degrees *per literas Regias* or letters mandatory should be issued by the Crown only on receipt of a petition from the Chancellor, who should not petition until he had received a certificate signed by a majority of the Heads of Houses in favour of the applicant. During the sixty years 1689–1748 of the Chancellorship of Charles Seymour (1662–1748), sixth Duke of Somerset, the comparatively moderate number of about seventy mandate degrees were conferred. Honorary degrees, though sometimes given at Royal visits, for example the sixteen Masters of Arts and one Doctor of Divinity at Queen Elizabeth's visit in 1564, are quite different from mandate degrees. In 1681, on the petition of Brady, then Regius Professor, who was concerned about the conditions under which the degree of Bachelor of Medicine was allowed, the Faculties of Law and Physic were placed on the same footing by a King's letter dated April 8, 1681.

REFERENCES

CHAPLIN, A. *Proc. Roy. Soc. Med.* 1920, XIII (Sect. Hist. Med.), 99.

Grace Book A, p. xxviii, edited by STANLEY LEATHES, for the Cambridge Antiquarian Society; Luard Memorial Series, Part I, Cambridge, 1897.

Grace Book Δ, p. xii, edited by J. VENN, Cambridge, 1910.

MACALISTER, A. *The History of the Study of Anatomy at Cambridge*, 1891.

—— *Brit. Med. Journ.* 1904, ii, 1094.

ORNSTEIN, M. *The Rôle of Scientific Societies in the Seventeenth Century*, p. 240, University of Chicago Press, 1928.

OSLER, W. *Thomas Linacre*, Cambridge, 1908.

PAYNE, J. F. Introduction to *Galeni Pergamensis de Temperamentis ...Libri Tres Thoma Linacro Anglo Interprete*, p. 301, Cambridge, 1881.

TANNER, J. R. *Historical Register of the University of Cambridge to the Year 1910*, Cambridge, 1917.

VENN, J. and J. A. *Alumni Cantabrigienses*, Part I, from the Earliest Times to 1900, in 4 volumes, Cambridge, 1922–1927.

The least satisfactory period of the University was the eighteenth century, of which Peacock in 1841 painted a very dark picture:

The corruption which had characterized and disgraced the government of the last century, and which had filled the colleges with fellows, who were neither distinguished by learning nor high principle, exerted a paralysing influence upon those who might otherwise have been disposed or able to restore the fallen studies and degraded character of the Universities.

It was, as Winstanley remarks, "by no means unknown for a newly appointed professor to be unacquainted with the rudiments of the subject he was supposed to teach". Richard Watson (1737–1816), in many ways a very favourable specimen of the professor of the period, confessed that when elected to the chair of chemistry in 1764 he knew nothing at all about the subject and that it was only by much hard work as his "other avocations would permit" that he was able fifteen months later to deliver a course of lectures; in justice to him it should be added that his *Chemical Essays* (1781) in five volumes, of which Sir Humphry Davy (1778–1829) said in 1813 that he could scarcely imagine a time, or a condition of the science, when they would be superannuated, went into a seventh edition. Others got out of the difficulty by not lecturing at all, and the average college tutor was not more conscientious than most of the professors. Richard Davies, M.D., F.R.S., fellow of Queens', in a letter dated 1759 advocating equipment with instruments as well as with books wrote: "the Arts subservient to Medicine have no appointments to encourage teachers in them. Anatomy, botany, chemistry and pharmacy have been but occasionally taught when some person of superior talents has sprung up and has honoured the University by his first display of them there before his passage into the world". John Edwards (1637–1716), fellow of St John's (1659), commented very severely on the conditions at Cambridge in the time of Queen Anne: "I might observe how our Religious Mammonists grasp at anything where gain is to be had. They fetch both Physic and Surgery under their jurisdiction". Though, as Trevelyan remarks, "The slumbers of the English Universities in the eighteenth century were more scandalous than the lighter and more broken slumbers of the Church". Cambridge did not escape the general moral and political deterioration of the country following the Restoration (1660), and particularly in the middle of the century corruption and benefice-seeking were common; the results of examinations were so biassed by favouritism that "when the Johnians had the disposal of honours, the second wrangler was always looked upon as the first". The University was controlled partly by the Elizabethan Statutes, partly by the *Statuta antiqua* not repealed by the Elizabethan Statutes, partly by Royal letters accepted by the University, and partly by Ordinances passed by Graces of the Senate; but the Senate could not modify the Elizabethan Statutes or the Royal letters. The senior members of the University had its control in their hands; the heads of colleges were vested with extraordinary powers, for they chose the Vice-Chancellor and had a large share in constituting the *Caput*. The complicated position can best be explained by the following quotation from Winstanley's clear account:

Before a Grace could be submitted to the Senate...it had to be unanimously approved by a small committee of that body, known as the *Caput* and consisting of the Vice-Chancellor, sitting *ex officio*, three doctors representing respectively the faculties of divinity, medicine, and law, a regent master of arts and a non-regent master of arts. A single member of the *Caput* had the right of vetoing a Grace, and this power of obstruction was the less defensible as belonging to a non-representative body. Though the *Caput* was annually elected, only Heads of Houses, doctors, and the two Scrutators were entitled to vote; and, restricted as were the electors, they were not even allowed an unfettered choice. At the beginning of the Michaelmas Term, which was the date appointed for the election of the *Caput*, the Vice-Chancellor and the two Proctors presented separate lists, each containing the names of three doctors in the different faculties and of a regent and a non-regent, and the choice of the electors was confined to the fifteen persons thus named. Further restrictions were imposed by custom. "Much depends in the election of a *Caput* on the prospect of the Vice-Chancellor for the ensuing year", wrote the Master of Corpus in 1764, "as by the usage of the University one is always of his own College and the rest usually such as are not thought disagreeable to him"; and according to another authority it was customary to vote for those whose names appeared on the Vice-Chancellor's list.

The age of reform had hardly begun to dawn. In the last quarter of the century the total number of undergraduates had fallen to under 400; and Medicine shared in the general depression.

There were, however, factors which might well have led to medical activity and research; the influence of Isaac Newton (1642–1727) and of Richard Bentley (1662–1742), the turbulent Master of Trinity, was in favour of science. On February 10, 1703, J. F. Vigani (1650?–1712), a native of Verona, who had taught chemistry for twenty years, was elected to the new chair in that subject, thus anticipating by exactly a century the establishment of a corresponding professorship at Oxford; in 1705 Bentley, much against the wishes of the senior fellows, provided Vigani with laboratory space in Trinity College; this room, previously the fifteenth century audit chamber of King's Hall and now the bursary of Trinity, may also be regarded as the first physiological laboratory, for Stephen Hales (1677–1761), having had a sound training in Newtonian physics, began experimental work there before he left Cambridge to become perpetual curate of Teddington, Middlesex, in 1708–9. During this century other chairs, those of anatomy, botany (November 10, 1724), and natural experimental philosophy (Jacksonian, 1783) were established; the last was founded with a great latitude in the choice of the subjects to be lectured on, but chemistry was specially mentioned and the professor was requested to "have an eye more particularly to that *opprobrium medicorum* called the gout". In 1707 the University founded the professorial chair in anatomy, but the first occupant, George Rolfe, appointed on June 21 of that year, was deprived of his office in 1728 for continued absence.

Though the eighteenth was the most stagnant of the last four centuries of Cambridge medicine, and the Regius Professors of Physic—Green, Plumptre, and Pennington—never taught regularly, some lectures were delivered by others: Richard Bradley (*obiit* Nov. 5, 1732), F.R.S., the first Professor of Botany (1724–1732), lectured in 1729 upon "the Materia Medica in the Physick Schools at Cambridge in the Collections of Dr Addenbroke and Signor J. F. Vigani" deposited in St Catharine's Hall and Queens' College; there is preserved in the Botany School his manuscript of "A Course of Botanical Lectures explaining the Principles of Vegitation", but undated. Bradley, however, whose entire ignorance of Latin and Greek caused considerable scandal, neglected his duties, and accordingly John Martyn (1699–1768), of Emmanuel, professor from 1733 to 1761, began to lecture in 1727 but ceased to do so in 1735. John Martyn was a medical man, practising in London a good deal between 1730 and 1752, and translated into English from the Latin Boerhaave's *Treatise on the Powers of Medicines* (1740) and Walter Harris's *Acute Diseases of Infants* (1742); he founded the botanical library and herbarium, and was succeeded by his son Thomas (1735–1825), of Sidney Sussex College, who occupied the chair for sixty-three years (1762–1825), but ceased to lecture in 1796, as his presentation of the subject did not arouse any enthusiasm, and after 1798 did not reside in Cambridge. J. S. Henslow (1796–1861), of St John's College, however, who followed him as professor (1825–1861), made the pursuit of botany extremely popular. William Heberden the elder (1710–1801), Linacre lecturer (1734–8) at St John's, gave an annual course of lectures in the Anatomical School for about ten years before he migrated to London in 1748, his tract "'Αντιθηριακά: an essay on Mithridatium and Theriaca" (1745) containing the substance of one of the lectures; in 1751 his pupil Robert Glynn, later Clobery (1719–1800), followed his example of lecturing regularly. Two of Heberden's other pupils, George Baker (1722–1809),

William Heberden.

WILLIAM HEBERDEN THE ELDER, M.D., F.R.S.

who proved that Devonshire colic and *colica Pictonum* were forms of lead poisoning, and Thomas Gisborne (1726–1806) were alternately Presidents of the Royal College of Physicians of London during the period 1785 to 1804. Until Haviland's time the most that the Regius Professors did in the way of lecturing was the delivery at the end of the formal physic Act of a "determination" or speech in Latin on the subject, a duty which did not occur more than four times a year.

On October 1, 1750, at the Quarterly Comitia of the Royal College of Physicians of London the dispute with the Universities of Oxford and Cambridge arising out of the intention of the College to admit to the fellowship graduates of foreign Universities was finally and amicably settled in favour of the Universities by the decision that no person should be admitted as a fellow of the College unless he was a Doctor of Physic of one of the English Universities.

REFERENCES

DAVIES, R. *The General State of Education in the Universities with a particular view to the Philosophical and Medical Education, set forth in an Epistle to Dr Hales, being Introductory to Essays on the Blood*, Bath, 1759.

EDWARDS, J. Quoted by Henry Bradshaw. *Camb. Antiquar. Communications*, 1879, III, 119.

PEACOCK, G. *Observations on the Statutes of the University of Cambridge*, p. 70 (note), London, 1841.

TREVELYAN, G. M. *History of England*, p. 521, London, 1929.

WINSTANLEY, D. A. *The University of Cambridge in the Eighteenth Century*, Cambridge, 1922.

WORDSWORTH, C. *Scholae Academicae, Some Account of the Studies at the English Universities in the Eighteenth Century*, pp. 116, 172, Cambridge, 1877.

In 1814 Dyer, the friend of Charles Lamb, expressed the
opinion general at the time by the statement that Cambridge had never been considered the proper place for
medical or anatomical students, who ought to go to some
great city such as London or Edinburgh. But Haviland's
appointment to the Regius chair in 1817, at the early age
of thirty-two, was followed by changes which led up to
the epoch-making reforms and advances that characterized
the nineteenth century as regards the medical school. In
1819 he began a course of fifty lectures a year on special
and general pathology and clinical medicine. On
February 27, 1829, the Senate at his instigation passed a
Grace which broke new ground; it obliged the candidates
to bring certificates that they had studied medicine at a
hospital for at least two years if they were away from
Cambridge, made attendance on lectures compulsory,
and improved the examinations for the M.B. degree.
The professors of anatomy, botany, and chemistry were
made examiners in addition to the Regius Professor who
had previously been the sole judge of a candidate's
qualifications for a medical degree, and the examinations
were conducted by written papers in English instead of a
Latin oral, and were held every term. It was further
decreed that the Downing Professor of Medicine should
give a course of fifty lectures on a subject not previously
covered by the Regius and the professors of chemistry,
botany, and anatomy.

A Grace on April 1, 1841, directed that candidates for
the licence *ad practicandum in Medicinâ* (M.L.) should

bring evidence of three years' hospital practice in addition to the nine terms of residence. In 1842 a practical clinical examination of patients was introduced into the final M.B. examination; this was the first time that this had been done in the United Kingdom and thus set an example which has been universally followed.

In 1848 after much discussion two new triposes, Moral Sciences and Natural Sciences, were established, the first examinations being held in the Lent Term of 1851. For the first twelve years the number of names in the class lists of the Natural Sciences Tripos never reached double figures, the yearly average being five. In 1876 the names in each class were arranged in alphabetical order, having previously been placed in order of merit. In 1881 the tripos was divided into Parts I and II, and in that transitional year there were nine names in the class list of the first part, one being that of a woman for the first time. In the following year the class list of Part I contained the names of sixty-two men and six women; in Part II there were six names, none in the first class.

The first Royal Commission, appointed on August 31, 1850, to inquire into the state, discipline, studies, and revenues of the University of Cambridge, the extraneous interference of which met with much remonstrance and not least from William Whewell (1794–1866), the forcible Master of Trinity, took a good deal of evidence about the position of Medicine; this showed that, though the total number of undergraduates in the University was 1500, in the previous ten years the average number of M.B. degrees conferred annually had not been more than four, and that the number of licentiates (M.L.) and M.D.s had been even lower. The licence to practise was not essential for the M.B. or M.D. degrees; it could be taken by M.A.s only, and two years after that degree. Between 1818 and 1834 it was taken by nine members of the University and mainly by residents, because some colleges did not allow M.B.s or M.D.s to be elected fellows. The licences M.L. and C.L. (the latter apparently not having been conferred after 1760) were abolished in 1859. The publication of this Commission's report, dated August 30, 1852, and the subsequent Statutory or Executive Commission (1856) were followed by considerable changes.

The establishment of an additional professorship of anatomy was recommended and carried into effect (*vide* p. 64). The institution of medical scholarships was advised as the best means of establishing a medical school, and it was suggested that the Linacre funds might be utilized for this purpose, a proposition not carried into effect, though the sale of the property in 1865 for £4185 would have made it possible to have done something in this direction at St John's College. Christopher Tancred (1689–1754), "the founder of useful charities", had by his will endowing studentships in physic at Gonville and Caius, as well as those in divinity and law, set an example in this respect. A Syndicate appointed on February 2, 1853, and continued on May 26 of the same year, to consider "whether it is expedient to adopt any measures, and if so what, for augmenting the existing means of teaching the students of the University by Public Professors and Public Lecturers", reported on March 27, 1854, on the conditions of graduation in Medicine and the studies and examinations of the students in that faculty;

their recommendations were approved by Grace of May 2. A Board of Medical Studies was established; Bachelors of Medicine were to rank as Masters of Arts; and in order to encourage students in Medicine to compete for honours in the Natural Sciences Tripos it was ordained that students obtaining honours in that tripos should be excused further examination in botany, comparative anatomy, physics, and chemistry in their medical course. The Commission legislated against the predominant power of the Heads of the Colleges in University affairs, and substituted the Council of the Senate for the autocratic "Caput" (*vide* p. 16). The interval between the M.B. and M.D. degrees was reduced from five to three years, and instead of two Acts for the M.D. degree one was made necessary. On August 11, 1854, the Royal Assent was given to an Act to extend to the graduates of the University of London the rights enjoyed by the graduates of Oxford and Cambridge in respect to the practice of physic.

On May 20, 1858, the Ordinance that theses for degrees should be in Latin was altered to the effect that "the candidate shall read a thesis composed in English by himself". In the following year candidates for the licence to practise physic were required to present evidence of five years' medical study unless they had an Arts' degree, in which case four years were sufficient. The examination for the M.B. was divided into two parts, the subjects for the first being chemistry, botany, comparative anatomy, human anatomy and physiology, pathology, materia medica and pharmacy, and selected passages from the medical classics—Hippocrates, Galen, and Aretaeus—

and for the second, medicine; but even in 1861 surgery and midwifery were not included and certificates for attendance on surgical teaching were not required.

From an analysis made by Arnold Chaplin, M.D., Harveian Librarian of the Royal College of Physicians of London, it may be interesting at this point to quote the following figures: between 1500 and 1856 the total number of Cambridge medical graduates was 1515, an average of four a year; of these 527 proceeded from Arts to Medicine, and 988, including two Regius Professors (Plumptre and Bond), proceeded to Medicine without a degree in Arts. The Colleges with the largest number of medical graduates were: Caius 225, St John's 179, Trinity 149, Emmanuel 94, Christ's 92, Queens' 75, Pembroke 73, King's 69, Jesus 66, Peterhouse 58, St Catharine's 53.

After the Lent term of 1860 the Natural Sciences Tripos qualified for the B.A. degree; before that time candidates were required to have passed a separate examination for the B.A. degree. In 1860–1 the degree of Master of Surgery (M.C.) was established, the abbreviation of which was after the war of 1914–18 changed to M.Chir. in order to avoid confusion with M.C., the Military Cross; at the same time the abbreviation B.C. for the degree of Bachelor of Surgery, which was established by Grace of February 1, 1883, was altered to B.Chir. In the year 1930–1 the examination for the Master in Surgery (M.Chir.), which had previously taken place twice a year at the same time as the M.B., B.Chir. examination in surgery, midwifery, and gynaecology, was arranged to be held once a year, in the Lent term. On March 22, 1866, a

24

Grace enacted that there should be three examinations for the M.B.; the first consisted of chemistry, physics, and comparative anatomy, for which schedules were given, the second of human anatomy, physiology, and materia medica, and the third of the clinical subjects.

In 1870 the Royal College of Surgeons of England, probably as a result of the influence of Humphry, who was on its Council from 1864 to 1884, recognized attendance at lectures on botany, chemistry, materia medica, anatomy, and physiology given at Cambridge as excusing candidates from their examination for the diploma of M.R.C.S. This year is memorable for the appointment as Praelector of Physiology at Trinity College of Michael Foster (*vide* p. 79) who created the Cambridge school of physiology and thus exerted an all-important influence on the modern development of the Medical School. A sign of the growing interest in natural science was the foundation on March 10, 1872, of the Cambridge University Natural Science Club, among the original nine members of which was Michael Foster's first demonstrator, Newell Martin (*vide* p. 79). The list of subsequent members, which at its thousandth meeting on January 24, 1920 contained 330 names (55 or 16.7 per cent. with F.R.S.), includes many well known in scientific medicine, such as J. G. Adami, Henry Head, Almroth Wright, Walter M. Fletcher (the secretary of the Medical Research Council), H. H. Dale, and T. R. Elliott.

In the academic year 1872–3, the medical and surgical degrees conferred were M.D.s 2, M.C.s 2, and M.B.s 6. In June 1873 nine candidates got through the first M.B., and the three examiners for the third M.B. approved three candidates. In the academic year 1874–5 the number of M.D.s conferred reached double figures (ten) for the first time. The two Inspectors of the General Council of Medical Education and Registration reported on the three parts of the M.B. examination in December 1874 in extremely favourable terms; for the first M.B. in chemistry, botany, heat and electricity, mechanics and hydrostatics, there were sixteen candidates; for the second examination in pharmacology, comparative anatomy, physiology, and human anatomy, twelve candidates; and for the third examination in medical jurisprudence (one paper), pathology and the practice of physic (two papers), four candidates. In the year 1878–9 the list of the Natural Sciences Tripos contained twenty-three names as compared with seventeen in 1870, but the number of medical degrees conferred remained small: M.D.s 2, M.C. 1, M.B.s 7. In the final examination for the M.B. degree in December 1877 the four examiners passed five candidates.

After the report of the Royal Commission on Oxford and Cambridge (1877–80) and the subsequent Statutes approved by the Queen in Council in 1882, the year 1883 saw a remarkable increase in the teachers of the ancillary sciences and the art of medicine; three new professorships, in physiology (Michael Foster), pathology (C. S. Roy), and surgery (G. M. Humphry), were founded; and by a Grace of December 6 the following University lectureships were established: in botany (Francis Darwin, 1848–1925), animal morphology (Adam Sedgwick, 1854–1913), three in physiology (W. H. Gaskell, J. N. Langley, and Sheridan Lea), in medicine (Donald MacAlister), surgery (G. E. Wherry), midwifery (R. N. Ingle), and medical jurisprudence (Bushell Anningson). On resigning the chair of anatomy Humphry offered to take without any stipend a chair of surgery, which the Special Board for Medicine had declared to be urgently necessary.

The establishment of lectureships in medicine (suppressed as from October 1, 1911), surgery (suppressed as from December 31, 1911), midwifery (suppressed by Grace of March 11, 1909), and medical jurisprudence (vacant since 1916) reflects Humphry's cherished ideal of a complete medical school at Cambridge, at any rate for those who needed it. But this opinion is contrary to that generally held. The available number of patients at Addenbrooke's Hospital is quite inadequate for the proper instruction of more than a very small proportion of the medical students, who now go to London or to some other large city for their clinical instruction. There are about 500 medical students in Cambridge doing pre-clinical work, and about the same number are engaged in clinical work elsewhere; the number of beds in Addenbrooke's Hospital is 200 and in a few years' time will be raised to 300, but even then the clinical material would be quite insufficient for such a large number of students. What might with great advantage be done at Cambridge is the institution of an advanced post-graduate Research Hospital, for a small number of men devoting their whole time to clinical science. While working at elementary pharmacology and general pathology for the third part of the second M.B., students are introduced to the elements of clinical work by attendance at Addenbrooke's Hospital, mainly in small batches with individual members of the staff.

The number of men going in for Medicine increased after 1883; thus in the academic year 1886–7 the number of entries for the second M.B. was 128 as compared with just under 100 in the year 1883–4. In the latter academic year the number of medical degrees conferred was M.D.s 10, M.B.s 26, and B.C.s 8, whereas in the year 1886–7 there were M.D.s 8, M.C. 1, M.B.s 49, and B.C.s 23.

A Grace of November 26, 1885, decided that students desiring admission to the first professional examination for the degree of M.B. should not be required by the University to be registered by the Registrar of the General Council of Medical Education and Registration. The Medical Act of 1886 ruled that in future no person should be registered under the Medical Acts who has not passed a qualifying examination in medicine, surgery, and midwifery. Accordingly changes were made by the Grace of April 28, 1887 in the University regulations governing the final examination for the M.B., B.C. degrees; subjects, such as surgical operations and appliances, which had previously been confined to the examination for the B.C., were included in that for the M.B., successful candidates being able to proceed forthwith to the B.C. degree and, after reading a thesis, to that of M.B. Further, the wording of the regulation that three years' attendance on the medical practice of a recognized hospital was required for the M.B. degree and two years' surgical practice for the degree of B.C. was altered to three years' medical and surgical practice at a recognized hospital for the degrees of M.B., B.C. The B.Chir. has therefore been a complete qualification in medicine, surgery and midwifery, entitling to registration. In accordance with the recommendation of the General Council of Medical Education and Registration that the course of medical education should occupy at least five years if elementary physics, chemistry, and biology are included in that period, or at least four years after a satisfactory examination in these subjects has been passed, a change was made in the University regulations for the degrees of M.B., B.C. Previously the period of medical study required before admission to the final examination for these degrees was five years, except for students who had taken honours in any tripos; but, as a matter of fact, very few students obtained the M.B. degree in less than five years. The exempting clause was expunged so that five years' medical study was required from all candidates. At the same time the examination in pharmacy and pharmaceutical chemistry forming part of the second M.B., which had not been satisfactory, was altered both in character and name. It was made more practical, dispensing was deferred to the final M.B. examination, and the name of the examination was changed to Pharmaceutical Chemistry.

In January 1888 the University presented a petition to the Queen in Council against the petition of the Royal College of Physicians of London and the Royal College of Surgeons of England begging that they should as a Senate of Physicians and Surgeons be empowered to grant degrees in Medicine and Surgery.

In the academic year 1891–2 the number of medical degrees conferred had gone up very considerably, namely M.D.s 19, M.B.s 72, and B.C.s 70.

Until 1892 the Regius Professors of Physic had been previous residents in Cambridge, and since 1785 physicians to Addenbrooke's Hospital. But Allbutt, when appointed Regius Professor in 1892, was not given access to the hospital, and it was not until March 1900 that this anomaly was corrected.[1] An arrangement was then made between the University and Addenbrooke's Hospital that in consideration of £300 paid annually out of the University Chest to the Treasurer of the hospital the governors of the hospital should, on the application of the Vice-Chancellor, elect the Regius Professor of Physic to be a physician, and the Professor of Surgery, if any, to be a surgeon, of the hospital, and assign to them a proportionate share of the beds or, if this was not required, facilities for teaching there. In addition, all proper facilities for the clinical parts of the third M.B. examinations were thus assured.

The great expansion of the Medical School made a corresponding increase of laboratory accommodation extremely urgent. In 1891 new buildings for anatomy and physiology were completed, but after a time the need for further buildings led to the appointment of a syndicate in 1899 and an appeal was organized by the Cambridge University Association. On March 1, 1904, the present Medical School in Downing Street, designed by E. S. Prior, which cost upwards of £34,000 and was planned to house the departments of medicine, surgery, midwifery,

[1] In 1889 Henry W. Acland (1815–1900), Regius Professor of Medicine (1858–1894) at Oxford, when thinking of his successor, suggested to the Radcliffe Infirmary that the future Regius Professor should *ex officio* have a certain number of beds under his charge; this did not meet with any support at the time, but William Osler from 1905 and his successors enjoyed this privilege.

pharmacology, and the Humphry Museum permanently, and to provide a home, it was hoped, temporarily, for the departments of pathology, public health, and medical jurisprudence, was opened by King Edward the Seventh and Queen Alexandra at the same time as the Law School and Squire Law Library, the Botanical School, and the Sedgwick Museum.

In 1902 P. W. Latham criticized the University teaching of medical students on the ground that about half only of those who began medical study obtained the M.B. degree. According to his figures rather more than a hundred medical students came into residence annually between 1888 and 1894, and the average time occupied in obtaining the M.B. degree was seven years from matriculation; but the average yearly number of degrees conferred between 1895 and 1901 was fifty-four. The total number of medical students in Cambridge in 1902, according to his estimate, was 394. The University records show that in the academic year 1901–2 there were 2658 undergraduates in residence.

An important change during the present century has been the great diminution in private coaching, for which students pay additional fees. An anonymous tract (ascribed to W. S. Powell [1717–1775], Master of St John's)—*An Observation on the Design of establishing annual Examinations at Cambridge* (1774)—advocated in the two previous years by John Jebb (1736–1786), M.D., F.R.S., of Peterhouse, speaks of private coaching as then frequent; in the last century this had greatly increased, so that in 1841 Peacock denounced private tuition as "an evil of the most alarming magnitude" which had "nearly absorbed every other mode of instruction in the University". Thus in the Mathematical Tripos it was the rule, and there were famous coaches, such as John Dawson (1734–1820) who, living at Sedbergh, counted twelve senior wranglers between 1781 and 1807 among his numerous pupils, William Hopkins (1793–1866), of Peterhouse, "the senior wrangler maker", who between January 1828 and January 1849 had taught 175 wranglers, of whom 17 had been senior, 44 among the first three, and 108 among the first ten wranglers (Wordsworth), and E. J. Routh (1831–1907), also of Peterhouse, who in the 31 years, 1858 to 1888, had 631 pupils most of whom were wranglers, and 27 senior wranglers (W. W. R. Ball). During the last fifteen years of the nineteenth, and even in the early years of the present century, there was a very considerable amount of private coaching in the sciences ancillary to medicine, chemistry, anatomy, and physiology. Thus in the Michaelmas term of 1893 E. Barclay-Smith, afterwards Professor of Anatomy at King's College, London, had a coaching class of 60 men in anatomy and physiology for the Natural Sciences Tripos, Part I, and on one occasion had a reading party of 70 during the Easter Vacation at Blankenberghe on the Belgian coast; he gave up these classes in 1897. The development of college teaching with the institution of supervisors, which began in 1896, gradually led to a great fall in the demand for private coaching.

After much discussion and many fly-leaves a Grace was passed on March 14, 1914, by 267 placets to 235 non-placets, authorizing an application to the Board of Education, by the University, on behalf of the

Special Board of Medicine, for a grant to the Medical Department.

On June 9, 1914, the new physiological laboratory, presented by the Drapers' Company, was opened by Prince Arthur of Connaught; this met an urgent need, as the number of students had reached nearly 300 and the research papers from the department occupied a yearly volume of 400 or more pages. The War then intervened, but the growing demands of biochemistry and the teaching of Gowland Hopkins, who had been Professor of Biochemistry since 1914, were met by the opening on May 9, 1924, by Lord Balfour, of the Sir William Dunn Biochemical Department which had cost about £100,000.

In 1921 the Molteno Institute for Research in Parasitology was opened by Lord Buxton and was placed under the direction of G. H. F. Nuttall, who had been Quick Professor of Biology since 1906. In 1928 a new laboratory for the Department of Pathology on the Downing Estate was opened; it also accommodated the Department of Animal Pathology.

In November 1919 a Royal Commission was appointed "to inquire into the financial resources of the Universities (of Oxford and Cambridge) and of the Colleges and Halls therein, into the administration and application of these resources, into the Government of the Universities, and into the relations of the Colleges and Halls to the Universities and to each other". On this Commission and in the business of the Medical School Hugh K. Anderson played a very important part. The Report appeared in March 1922, and tended to strengthen the Faculties as compared with the Colleges, and accordingly recommended that any Government grants should be made to the University and not to the Colleges. It regarded the old system of prize fellowships, which were held unconditionally for a term of years, as obsolete and destined to disappear, and stated that fellows must either render service to the Colleges or to knowledge in return for their emoluments. Retirement from official posts at an age limit and pensions on a contributory basis were recommended.

The following figures showing the entries for the Natural Sciences Tripos and for the examinations for Medical and Surgical Degrees in 1887 and in 1921, contained in Appendix XI of the Royal Commission's Report, are of interest as showing the increase in number of the science and medical students:

Natural Sciences Tripos	1887	1921
Part I	100	279
Part II	20	79
M.B. Examinations		
1st	381	456
2nd	303	357
3rd	112	254

In 1929–30 the total number of undergraduates, including Research Students, was 5671, of which 472 were women. In the Michaelmas term 1930 there were 498 male medical students in residence, or practically the same as the number (488) in the Michaelmas term of 1919, after the War. The number of medical degrees conferred in the academic year 1929–30 were M.D.s 27, M.Chir.s 3, M.B.s 56, and B.Chir.s 62. It is rather remarkable that this is much the same total as in the academic year 1902–3, when there were 23 M.D., 59 M.B., and 83 B.C. degrees conferred, although the total number of medical students was, according to P. W. Latham's estimate, 394.

With the great increase in the scope of the medical curriculum in recent years, rendering the medical student's burden far heavier and the number of examinations more numerous than in the last century, a change in the attitude of the Cambridge medical student to the Natural Sciences Tripos became obvious a few years after the war. Statistics prepared in 1930 show that in the period 1906–1911 (6 years) the percentage of medical students who took the Natural Sciences Tripos was seventy-seven, whereas in the period 1920–6 (seven years) it fell to forty-four. This had taken place in spite of circumstances which should have had the opposite effect, namely the increasing number of medical students who complete the whole or the greater part of the four parts of the first M.B. examination before coming into residence, and the larger number of colleges which require medical students to take the Tripos. Thus there is a danger that, just as the medical student has become less familiar with the "old humanities" so will he, in spite of being a member of this University, lose touch in the future with the bearings of the natural sciences on his technical activities. The advantages of a University over a medical school will thus be lost. A possible remedy proposed (*vide Cambridge University Reporter* 1931, LXI, 737) was that the number of examinations (*vide* p. 37) should be reduced by substituting a single examination for the first part of the Natural Sciences Tripos and the second M.B. examinations. Such an examination might be instituted by alterations in the Natural Sciences Tripos or in the second M.B. examinations, or by a fresh grouping of subjects to form a Medical Sciences Tripos. In any event the successful candidates in this examination should be exempt from further examination in the subjects of the second M.B., be qualified to proceed (*a*) to the degree of B.A., and (*b*) to proceed to one of the courses for Part II of the Natural Sciences Tripos.

A Grace of April 24, 1931 appointed a Syndicate to consider the medical courses and examinations of the University and their relations to courses and examinations for the degree of B.A.

REFERENCES

Cambridge University Reporter.

BALL, W. W. R. *A History of the Study of Mathematics at Cambridge*, p. 163, Cambridge, 1889.

DYER, G. *History of the University and Colleges of Cambridge*, I, 219, London, 1814.

Historical Register of the University of Cambridge to the Year 1910, edited by J. R. TANNER, Cambridge,1917; *Supplement* 1910–1920, edited by G. V. C. 1922.

PEACOCK, G. *Observations on the Statutes of the University of Cambridge*, London, 1841.

SHIPLEY, A. E. "*J*." *A Memoir of John Willis Clark*, London, 1913.

—— *Christopher Tancred, A Neglected Benefactor*. Printed for Private Circulation, Cambridge, 1925.

WILLIS and CLARK. *Architectural History of the University of Cambridge*, III, 145–90, Cambridge, 1886.

EXAMINATIONS FOR MEDICAL AND
SURGICAL DEGREES

With the advance of knowledge and of medical education, the number and scope of the examinations have steadily increased. There are three examinations which are so subdivided that there are in all nine class lists in which the names of candidates must appear before they are qualified to take the B.Chir. degree and keep the Act for the M.B. degree.

The first M.B. examination consists of four parts: (i) chemistry, general and inorganic, (ii) mechanics, (iii) physics, and (iv) elementary biology. The examinations are held three times a year. These separate parts can be passed singly or at the same time, and can with great advantage be completed before the student comes into residence. If this is not done, work for the Natural Sciences Tripos and for the second M.B. is necessarily delayed. Exemption from the first M.B. is allowed to those who have passed a number of similar examinations at Licensing Bodies and other Universities, approved by the Faculty Board of Medicine.

The second M.B. examination consists of three parts. (i) Organic chemistry which, like the four parts of the first M.B. examination, can be passed by a student before coming into residence. There are three examinations during the year. Exemption from this examination can be obtained by a candidate who has attained a sufficiently high standard in that subject in the Natural Sciences Tripos. (ii) Human anatomy and physiology. For this, among other requirements, "a certificate of having practised dissection during not less than one academic year and of having dissected the entire body" is necessary. The examination takes place twice a year. Exemption from the physiological part of this examination is granted to a student who has attained a sufficiently high standard in this subject in the Natural Sciences Tripos, but he then has to attain a higher standard in human anatomy than that required of candidates presenting themselves for examination in both subjects. (iii) Elementary pharmacology, including pharmaceutical chemistry, and the elements of general pathology. Before admission to this examination, candidates must have passed parts i and ii of the second M.B. examination, and produce certificates of attendance on courses in the subjects named and in elementary medicine or surgery. This latter is all the clinical work that the vast majority of medical students do while in residence at Cambridge. The examination is held twice a year.

The third M.B. examination consists of two parts which may be taken together or separately. (i) The principles and practice of surgery (including special pathology) and midwifery and diseases peculiar to women. In 1929 a practical examination in midwifery and gynaecology was introduced. Candidates must have completed five calendar years (certificates of at least nine months' study in each calendar year being required) of medical study, and have passed all the parts of the second M.B. examination. (ii) Principles and practice of physic (including diseases of children, mental diseases, and medical jurisprudence); pathology (including hygiene and preventive medicine), and pharmacology (including therapeutics and toxicology).

After the nine examinations have been passed the degree of
B.Chir., which is a double qualification for practice, can
be taken at once. There is a special Congregation for
medical degrees in the Long Vacation, so that candidates
who have passed their last examination in June after the
last Congregation in the Easter term can proceed then to
their degrees. For the degree of M.B. the candidate must
write a thesis on a subject approved by the Regius
Professor who accepts anatomical, physiological, biochemical, pathological, surgical, obstetrical, and gynae-
cological titles as well as those of purely medical topics.
If the thesis when written is also approved, the Act is
kept before the Regius Professor or his deputy in the
following manner: the candidate reads his thesis or such
part of it as he is directed to do; the Regius Professor or
his deputy then brings forward arguments or objections
for the candidate to answer, and examines him orally on
questions connected with his thesis. This public Act
interferes with the possible activity of "Ghosts" who,
at any rate in past centuries, have earned a somewhat
precarious living by writing theses for candidates who are
willing to sacrifice their financial and moral capital in
order to save themselves trouble. Cambridge is the only
University which requires a thesis for the degree of M.B.
and has done so not so much as part of the examination
as a means of education. The inaugural thesis is a survival
or rather a continuation of the disputations which long
ago formed the whole or a large part of the examinations
for degrees. This intellectual exercise appears to have been

formally initiated by St Bonaventure (1221–1274), the Italian Cardinal and Superior of the Franciscan Order, with the object of controlling the instruction given by teachers and of testing the progress made by students; in 1266 St Bonaventure sustained a thesis at Paris. In the fourteenth century these disputations formed part of the obligations for the degree of *Magister Artium* at the Sorbonne, Paris. The writing of a thesis obliges the candidate to think, stimulates him to report logically and intelligibly on what he has observed and done, and is often the first piece of literary composition that the candidate has taken seriously.

Most Cambridge men take the diploma of the Conjoint Examining Board of the Royal Colleges of Physicians and of Surgeons in England before proceeding to the degree of M.B. and B.Chir., and indeed often before entering for the final M.B., B.Chir. examination. A return, made out by the General Council of Medical Education and Registration of the United Kingdom, giving the qualification on which registration was first made in the years 1927–1930, showed that during these four years there were twenty medical practitioners whose first registration was on the Cambridge degree.

Degree of M.D. The candidate must compose a thesis on a subject approved by the Regius Professor of Physic. The thesis, of which four copies must be sent in, is considered by the M.D. Committee and, if it is approved, the candidate writes an extempore essay and keeps the Act in public before the Regius Professor and his Assessor. No person may present a thesis or dissertation for the degree of M.D. unless he has already been admitted Bachelor of

Medicine or Master of Arts or of Surgery. A Master of Surgery is excused the essay for the M.D. A Bachelor of Medicine may be admitted Doctor of Medicine in the ninth term after the term in which he was admitted Bachelor of Medicine. A Master of Arts may be admitted Doctor of Medicine in the twelfth term after that in which he was created or admitted Master of Arts. But this regulation does not apply to the date at which the Act for the degree is kept; in other words, the Act may be kept long before the degree can be taken.

The *M.D. Committee*, consisting of the Regius Professor of Physic and his Assessor, the Professor of Pathology and three members of the Faculty Board of Medicine appointed annually by that Board, was constituted in 1910 and came into force in the Lent term 1911. Up till that date the Regius Professor and his Assessor were responsible for adjudication of the M.D. theses.

Degrees in Medicine in absentiâ. A candidate who, having fulfilled all the other conditions for the degree of M.B. or M.D., is unable on account of absence abroad to keep the Act in person may apply through the Registrary to the Regius Professor of Physic for permission to present instead a dissertation on some subject approved by the Regius Professor. If the permission is granted, the dissertation (four copies in the case of the M.D.) with any memoir or other work on a medical subject published by him, which he may desire to submit, is then sent in for consideration by the M.D. Committee. This regulation came into force in 1905.

The *Raymond Horton-Smith Prize*, founded in January 1900 in memory of Raymond John Horton-Smith (1873–

1899), M.A., M.B., is awarded to the candidate for the degree of M.D. who presents the best thesis during the year. The value of the prize is about £20.

Master of Surgery (M.Chir.). Masters of Arts may be admitted to this examination after they are legally qualified to practise surgery. Candidates who are not Masters of Arts may be admitted to the examination when two years have elapsed after they have completed all that is required for the degree of Bachelor of Surgery; but no such student shall be admitted to the degree of Master of Surgery until three years have elapsed since he was admitted Bachelor of Surgery. The examination, formerly held twice a year at the same time as the first part of the third M.B. examination, has since the beginning of 1931 been held once a year in the Lent Term.

After a Grace of October 20, 1921, was passed to confer the titles of degrees by diploma on duly qualified women, the first occasion on which a woman received a diploma for the titular degree of M.B. was in May 1925, and for the degree of M.D. in December 1930. It may be mentioned here that on April 10, 1916, the Mistress of Girton and the Principal of Newnham applied to the Vice-Chancellor in order to gain admission to the first and second M.B. examinations for their students who, without this, were at a grave disadvantage when applying for admission to other medical examinations. A Report of the Special Board for Medicine, dated October 18, recommended this concession, and Grace of November 18, 1916, approved the admission of women to the first and second M.B. examinations under conditions similar to those under which they are admitted to the Previous and Tripos Examinations.

Cambridge has given a much wanted lead by establishing medical diplomas in special subjects which have been open to others than graduates of the University.

The first *Diploma in Public Health* (D.P.H.) in the country was established by a Grace of the Senate on February 4, 1875; this example was widely followed by other Universities and licensing bodies, such as that given conjointly by the Royal College of Physicians of London and the Royal College of Surgeons of England since 1888. In 1913–14 there were 118 entries for the Cambridge Diploma, and the same number in 1920–21. The London School of Hygiene and Tropical Medicine, which was formally opened on July 18, 1929, supplied facilities for this teaching, and as a result the number of men taking the course at Cambridge diminished and the diploma will cease in 1932.

A *Diploma in Tropical Medicine and Hygiene* was established by a Grace of the Senate on January 28, 1904. In 1912 the Royal Colleges of Physicians and Surgeons jointly established a Diploma in Tropical Medicine and Hygiene. For the same reasons as in the case of the Diploma in Public Health this Cambridge diploma will also cease in 1932.

A *Diploma in Psychological Medicine* was established by a Grace of the Senate on May 23, 1912; nine years later a Diploma in Psychological Medicine was granted conjointly by the Royal Colleges of Physicians and Surgeons; in 1913–14 there were 7 and in 1920–21 14 entries. The Cambridge diploma was discontinued in 1927.

A *Diploma in Medical Radiology and Electrology* (D.M.R.E.) was established by a Grace of the Senate on June 17, 1919, and was the first of the kind in this country; in the year 1920–21 there were 69 entries. The example was followed by the University of Liverpool in 1920 and of Edinburgh in 1926.

The University is controlled by the Statutes, such as the *Statuta antiqua*, the Elizabethan Statutes of 1570, and those made as the result of the Royal Commissions of 1850, 1877, and 1919. It is difficult to make any general change in the Statutes unless the case for reform is very strong. Complete revision of them involves, at any rate in modern times, a preliminary inquiry by a Royal Commission; thus the Statutes now current came into force in 1926, but the machinery which created them was set in motion in 1919. Sporadic amendments of particular Statutes occupy much less time in making; they originate in the University and become law on approval by the Crown in Council.

In addition to the Statutes there are the Ordinances of the University; according to Statute A, chapter VI, section 1, "The University shall have power, for the encouragement of learning, the maintenance of good order and discipline, and the management of its affairs, to enact ordinances, provided always that no such ordinance shall contravene any provision of the Statutes". With the exception of those for the performance of the functions still assigned to the Senate by Statute, the Ordinances are made by Graces submitted to the Regent House, which consists of certain classes of resident Members of the Senate. The procedure for amending such Ordinances is comparatively easy and short.

The *Statutes of the University*. The *Statuta antiqua*, or old statutes, which appear to have been formulated by the Senate between 1303 and 1506, were not arranged in any order, and as the addition of a fresh law was not accompanied by the repeal of former ones, they became confused and contradictory so as to justify the epithets of "antiquated, semi-barbarous, and unintelligible" applied to them in the Royal Letter accompanying the Statutes of Edward VI in 1549. They provided for the degrees of M.B. and M.D. and for the licences to practise medicine and surgery, and for the control of the Faculty in other respects (*vide* p. 3).

The *Edwardian Statutes* of 1549 (*vide* p. 8).

Cardinal Pole's Statutes (1557) which were chiefly remarkable for changes in the ancient forms of election of the Vice-Chancellor.

The *Elizabethan Statutes* of 1559 which made only slight changes in those of Edward VI.

The *Elizabethan Statutes* of 1570, in which Whitgift, Caius, and other Heads of Colleges are said to have had a share, superseded the *Statuta antiqua*, gave the Heads of the Colleges and the *Caput Senatus* despotic powers, and brought in changes of which, from a medical point of view, the most far-reaching was that medical students were no longer obliged to take a degree in Arts before obtaining that in Medicine (*vide* p. 10). These Statutes governed the University until 1855.

The *Royal Commissions* of 1850, 1877, and 1919, and the findings of the Statutory or Executive Commissions which dealt with the Reports of the Royal Commissions, led to final Statutes approved by the Crown in Council.

The changes in the medical curriculum due to new Statutes and Ordinances are mentioned in the chronological account of the Medical School (pp. 1–44).

II. *Department of Anatomy*

IN August 1565 John Caius, who was mainly responsible for the introduction of the study of practical
anatomy into England, obtained from Queen Elizabeth
a formal yearly grant of two bodies, of criminals or unknown strangers dying in Cambridge, for dissection in
Gonville and Caius College. His statutes of that college,
dated September 4, 1557, contain directions about the
care of these bodies. Until the chair of anatomy was
founded by the University in 1707, the Regius Professors
of Physic were responsible for the teaching of human
anatomy and were required to do one "anatomy" a year
by a decree of 1562, and to be fined if their duties were not
carried out. The Regius Professors of Physic, however,
did not escape reproach in this respect, for on January 28,
1627, within three months of John Collins's accession to
the chair, attention was called to their negligence and a
Grace was then passed to correct this; accordingly in the
following March an "anatomy" was held in the Regent
House, subsequently the Catalogue Room of the Library.
Again in 1646, when Glisson was Regius but much at
Colchester and away from Cambridge, an order was given
that the "Regius Reader in Physic" should resume his
anatomical demonstrations, and the neglect of his duty
"through a paltry economy" was severely condemned.
Dissections were occasionally carried out independently
of the Regius Professor, for example in Jesus College in

47

1631 (Macalister), and by Richard Watson, Professor of Chemistry, who in 1765 dissected in his laboratory a corpse obtained from London. Though in the seventeenth century the "anatomies" were usually carried out in the Regent House, they were sometimes performed in the Physic School on the ground floor of what was later the South Library.

During his forty-one years' (1636–1677) tenure of the Regius Professorship, Glisson, described by Boerhaave as the "most accurate of anatomists", stimulated the study of anatomy; though much away (*vide* p. 152) he seems to have attracted to Cambridge George Joyliffe (1621–1658), who in 1651 while at Oxford had observed the lymphatics and, though he never published this discovery, communicated it in 1652 to Glisson, who recorded it in his *Anatomia Hepatis* (1654). A number of men educated or incorporated at Cambridge subsequently became anatomists, such as Thomas Winston (1575–1655) of Clare, Thomas Wharton (1614–1673) of Pembroke, William Croone (1633–1684) of Emmanuel, Clopton Havers (*obiit* 1702) of St Catharine's, William Briggs (1642–1704) of Corpus, Edward Tyson (1650–1708) of Corpus, Humphrey Ridley (1653–1708) of Pembroke, and James Blake (1667–1708) of Caius. James Keill or Keil (1673–1719), a Scot, was an active supporter of the iatro-mathematical school of medicine, and the author of a number of physiological and anatomical works, among them an account in 1706 of the death and dissection of John Bayles, a button-maker of Northampton, reputed to be 130 years old; Keill lectured on anatomy both at Oxford and Cambridge before settling down to practise at

Northampton in 1703, he received the honorary degree of M.D. at Cambridge in 1705, and on March 20, 1711, was elected a fellow of the Royal Society. His death from a long-standing tumour in the mouth, probably a ranula, apparently caused some feeling about the treatment, for his medical attendant, John Rushworth, felt called upon to publish the details in 1719 (*vide A Collection of Chirurgical Tracts written and collected* by William Beckett, F.R.S. pp. 61–77, 1740). A notebook of a student, Thomas Jenyns of Clare Hall, began with the words "I went to an Italian anatomist at Cambridge on May 23, 1692"; but the name of the anatomist is not disclosed.

In the early eighteenth century, anatomy became more generally recognized as worthy of University teaching, and after the establishment of a professorship in 1707 at Cambridge the University of Dublin followed suit in 1711. The immediate effect, however, in Cambridge was disappointing as regards research or real teaching; for out of the first five professors three (Rolfe, Banks, and Gibson) appear to have been absentees, and another (Cuthbert) held the chair for one year only.

A new provision for the teaching of anatomy was made in 1716 when an anatomical lecture room, figured in Ackermann's *History of the University of Cambridge* (II, 290, London, 1815), and private rooms were assigned to the Professors of Anatomy (George Rolfe) and of Chemistry (John Waller (*obiit* 1718), B.D.). These were in the new part, erected in 1689, of the University Printing House, at the corner of Silver Street and Queens' Lane, opposite the entrance to Queens' College; this building was handed over because, in the words of the Grace, "it was of no use to the University for any other purpose". This arrangement proved to be quite inadequate and the Professor of Chemistry went elsewhere, the Professor of Anatomy being left to share the premises with the Regius Professors of Physic and Modern History. In 1833 accommodation consisting of a dodecagonal museum, a small dissecting room, a lecture theatre, and a private room for the Professor of Anatomy, and two rooms for the Professor of Chemistry, was provided for the departments of anatomy, physic, botany, chemistry, mineralogy, and applied mechanics, erected at a cost of £3630 on a site, later occupied by the Medical School (opened in 1904), at the corner of Downing Street and Corn Exchange Street, then known as Slaughter House Lane. This was the original site of the old "Physic Garden" (*vide* p. 132) from which the Botanic Garden was transferred between 1846 and 1852 to the present position between Trumpington Road and Hills Road. On the evening of December 2, 1833, this anatomical building, sometimes called the Rotunda, was attacked by a mob under the erroneous impression that Clark had failed to comply with the requirements of the Anatomy Act.

As a result of the establishment in 1848 of the Natural Sciences Tripos (the first examination being held in 1851), the need of more accommodation for the biological sciences became urgent, and from 1853 onwards this question was much discussed, effective action, however, being long delayed. Some changes were made from time to time, for example in 1861, and in 1865–6 removal of the specimens illustrating comparative anatomy to the new museum constructed for them left more room for human anatomy and chemistry. In 1876, mainly by Humphry's influence, human anatomy was recognized as a separate subject in the Natural Sciences Tripos. About 1885 the increased number of students made it necessary to erect a temporary iron building as a dissecting room; this was occupied until 1891 when a new anatomical department with a lecture room providing seating for 280 students was completed. The dodecagonal building, which since 1880 had been in bad repair and invaded by dry rot, was used for the teaching of surgery, obstetrics, and medico-legal medicine, and contained the pathological collection. It survived for fifteen more years, and was finally demolished in order to make room for the Medical School erected on the site and opened on March 1, 1904, by King Edward and Queen Alexandra.

The supply of subjects for dissection has almost always been an anxious problem. On February 24, 1723–4, a clause was suggested, but subsequently withdrawn, in a Parliamentary Bill to provide that the bodies of persons executed for felony or other crimes in the counties of Cambridge and Huntingdon should be available for anatomical teaching. In the eighteenth century and until the passing of Lord Warburton's Anatomy Act in 1832, which provided that all unclaimed bodies should under proper restrictions go to the medical schools, the body-snatchers or resurrectionists were the main source of supply. This course was not free from possible scandal and trouble, as shown by the discovery of Laurence Sterne's body in the dissecting room in 1768 (*vide* p. 61) and the attack by a Cambridge mob on the anatomical school in 1833. The demand has exceeded the supply to such an extent that twenty students are now commonly allocated to each body, and at times the only way of providing material for dissection has been the use of human foetuses, still-born infants, monkeys, or dogs. In 1910 the Licensed Teachers of Anatomy in the United Kingdom, under the chairmanship of Macalister, started concerted action and, after instituting an inquiry into the existing conditions of supply and demand, approached the Government in 1912 in order to obtain amendment of the Anatomy Acts. Nothing definite, however, was effected before or during the War, and in 1919 and 1920 there was a crisis in the widespread and very grave shortage of subjects; for example at Cambridge three adult bodies only were available for 280 students. In 1920 the Ministry of Health took over the administration of the Anatomy Acts in England and Wales and the responsibility not only of supervising the anatomy schools but of helping them to secure an adequate supply of the necessary material. Without any new legislation an organized scheme for insuring a supply was successfully instituted.

The anatomical collection of the University was built up by many hands. In 1804 Sir Isaac Pennington presented the specimens bought from Thomas Lawrence (1711–1785) who had been Anatomy Lecturer at Oxford (1745–1750) during the Regius Professorship (1730–1758) of W. Woodford, and also lectured on this subject at the corner of Lincoln's Inn Fields near Clare Market in London from 1743 to 1748. On April 24, 1804, an annual grant of ten pounds was made for the maintenance of this collection. After Sir Busick Harwood's death the University bought his collection in 1815 for £367 10s., and some of his, though none of Lawrence's, can now be identified from their labels. In 1819 the University obtained a series of Calanzuoli's wax models illustrating human anatomy, and in 1836 purchased the anatomical collection, consisting of 2000 specimens, of James Macartney (1776–1843), Professor of Anatomy and Chirurgery (1813–1837) in Trinity College, Dublin, for ten yearly payments of £100. Humphry was an indefatigable collector for the museum and bought and presented the collections of skulls made by Schroeder van der Kolk of Utrecht, and by John Thurnam (1810–1873). In October 1898 Professor Flinders Petrie presented nineteen cases of skulls and bones from his excavations at Hierakonpolis, Egypt, which, Professor Alexander Macalister considered, made the Cambridge collection of Egyptian anthropology not only the largest in Great Britain, but probably in Europe.

The chair of anatomy was established without any definite regulations as to its scope in 1707, and so could be taken to include that of animals as well as of man until 1866 when the University, after the Report of a Syndicate appointed on May 11, 1865, to consider the best mode of providing for the teaching of anatomy and zoology in the University, founded an additional professorship of zoology and comparative anatomy (*vide* p. 64). In 1920, however, by a Grace of March 12, the subjects assigned to the chair of anatomy were re-defined to include vertebrate anatomy and embryology as well as human anatomy.[1]   James Thomas Wilson, F.R.S.,

[1] At Oxford a praelectorship in anatomy was founded in 1624 by Richard Tomlins of Westminster who assigned it to the Regius

Challis Professor of Anatomy (1890–1920) in the University of Sydney, was appointed in this year. In the first 112 years of the chair there were eleven occupants, the tenancies of the office varying from one (Cuthbert) to forty-nine years (Clark). Six of the total twelve professors have been fellows of the Royal Society.

The stipend of the chair was £600 (or £400 if the Professor holds a Headship or Fellowship), exclusive of fees, until a Grace of March 12, 1920, fixed it at £850 with an additional sum of £350 from the funds of the department.

Professorship of Medicine. In 1750 Matthew Lee (1694–1755) established a Readership in Anatomy, with an annual stipend of £140, at Christ Church. In 1803 George Aldrich, D.M., of Merton, annexed the revenue (£130) of the chair of anatomy, which he had founded in 1798, to the Tomlins praelectorship and so to the Regius chair. According to H. W. Acland (*Oxford and Modern Medicine*, p. 14, 1890), there was hardly any anatomical teaching in 1844 when he became Lee's Reader. In 1858 the revenues of the Tomlins and Aldrich trusts were attached, by Statute approved by the Queen in Council, to the Linacre Professorship of Physiology. The University Commission of 1877 altered the designation of the chair to the Linacre Professorship of Human and Comparative Anatomy, the Waynflete Professorship of Physiology (of which Sir John Burdon-Sanderson (1828–1903) was the first occupant in 1883) being founded. In 1893 the title of the Linacre chair was again changed so as to confine its scope to comparative anatomy, and an extraordinary Professorship of Human Anatomy was created, which in 1919 was called Dr Matthew Lee's Professorship of Anatomy. The separation of comparative from human anatomy may be compared with the changes at Cambridge.

A *Readership in Human Anatomy* was established by Grace of November 26, 1920, and was filled by W. L. H. Duckworth of Jesus College who had previously been University Lecturer in Physical Anthropology (1899–1920).

A *University Lectureship in advanced Human Anatomy* with a stipend of £50 was established by Grace of November 8, 1888, but has been vacant since 1915.

A *University Lectureship in Embryology* was established by Grace of December 2, 1922.

Demonstrators of Human Anatomy. By Grace of February 8, 1866, a demonstratorship was established; the Grace of November 8, 1888, abolished this office and in its place created a senior and two junior demonstratorships, and by Grace of January 29, 1903, two additional demonstrators were appointed.

The second holder of the demonstratorship, from 1876 to 1878, was Charles Creighton (1847–1927), who placed the profession under a deep debt of obligation for his masterly *History of Epidemics in Britain from A.D.* 664, in two volumes (1891 and 1894), and was ostracized by orthodox medical opinion for his opposition to vaccination.

A. Marmaduke Sheild (1858–1922) of Downing College, and surgeon to St George's Hospital, London, left £91,000, the bulk of which, after a life interest, is to found a "Marmaduke Sheild" Scholarship and to be used for the general purposes of the Medical School of Cambridge.

REFERENCES

ALLEN, F. J. "Evolution of the Medical School at Cambridge," *Brit. Med. Journ.* 1920, i, 506.

MACALISTER, A. *The History of the Study of Anatomy in Cambridge*: A Lecture delivered January 29, 1891, on the Opening of the New Anatomical Lecture Room; Cambridge.

MACPHAIL, A. *Brit. Med. Journ.* 1922, ii, 788. (Administration of the Anatomy Act.)

WILLIS, R. and CLARK, J. W. *Architectural History of the University of Cambridge*, III, 133, 155–7, Cambridge, 1886.

PROFESSORS OF ANATOMY

	Appointed
George Rolfe	1707
John Morgan	1728
George Cuthbert	1734
Robert Banks	1735
William Gibson	1746
Charles Collignon	1753
Sir Busick Harwood	1785
John Haviland	1814
William Clark	1817
Sir George Murray Humphry	1866
Alexander Macalister	1883
John Thomas Wilson	1920

GEORGE ROLFE, M.D.

Professor of Anatomy 1707–1728

George Rolfe, who had previously taught anatomy for some years in Cambridge, was given the title of Professor of Anatomy on June 12, 1707. The available information about him is remarkably scanty; the dates of his birth and death are not known, and he was not a member of any college or a graduate of the University. The records of the Barber-Surgeons show that on March 9, 1695, a George Rolph was admitted to the Freedom, and that this was the future first professor of anatomy at Cambridge seems probable, as in April 1701 he advertised a course of lectures on anatomy at the Barber-Surgeons' Hall. He was then living at the upper end of Chancery Lane. According to Peachey he was the first definitely recorded private teacher of human anatomy in London, and continued to lecture there until 1713 at least. The neglect of professional duties so widespread later in the century at Cambridge was certainly shared by him; for after being sternly warned by a Grace passed on December 16, 1722, of what would happen unless he mended his ways, the long suffering University deprived him of his chair on April 17, 1728, for "continued absence for several years from his office". The following explanation is offered by Peachey: after the clause in a Parliamentary Bill for increasing the supply of subjects for dissection in the University of Cambridge was withdrawn in February 1723–4, popular prejudice became so strong that the difficulty in obtaining bodies for demonstration may have made it impossible for Rolfe to carry out his official duties. This perhaps would account for the absence of any reform on his part after the Grace of December 16, 1722. William Stukeley (1687–1765), the antiquary, who entered Corpus Christi College in 1703, worked under Stephen Hales, took the degree of M.B. in 1709, and in 1722 gave the Goulstonian Lectures at the Royal College of Physicians of London with the title "Of the Spleen: its Description and History, Uses and Diseases, with Observations on the Dissection of an Elephant", is stated to have "studied anatomy under Mr Rolfe, the surgeon" (Masters).

REFERENCES

MASTERS, R. *History of the College of Corpus Christi and the B. Virgin Mary, Cambridge*, p. 382, Cambridge, 1753.
PEACHEY, G. C. *A Memoir of William and John Hunter*, pp. 12–14, Plymouth, 1924.

JOHN MORGAN, M.A.
Professor of Anatomy 1728–1734

John Morgan, the second professor of anatomy, was born in 1702, the son of Edward Morgan of Goldgrove, Flintshire. In May 1718 he was admitted a pensioner of Trinity College, became a scholar in 1719, and was twenty-seventh in the *Ordo Senioritatis* of 1721–2. In 1724 he was elected a fellow of Trinity, and in 1728 Professor of Anatomy, a chair he held for six years. Macalister, though not finding any record of his work, points to indirect evidence, the activity of resurrectionists in the neighbourhood, that dissection was then diligently studied; according to R. Masters (*loc. cit.* p. 196)

the practice of digging up human bodies in the church yards of Cambridge and the neighbouring villages and carrying them into colleges to be dissected became more common about this time, although to the no small offence of all serious people, was now proceeded against and the disturbance which this scandalous practice caused between the scholars and the inhabitants was prevented.

To remedy this an Ordinance was passed on December 10, 1731.

GEORGE CUTHBERT, M.A.
Professor of Anatomy 1734–5

George Cuthbert was born at Newcastle-on-Tyne in 1706 as the son of John Cuthbert. Admitted a pensioner at Trinity College in April 1724 when 18 years old, he became a scholar in the following year, and proceeded to the degree of B.A. (1727–8) and M.A. (1731). He was elected a fellow of Trinity in 1730 and Professor of Anatomy in 1734, but held office for one year only.

ROBERT BANKS (1702–1746), M.D., F.R.C.P.
Professor of Anatomy 1735–1746

Robert Banks or Bankes was born on November 12, 1702, in St Mary-at-Hill, London, where his father, Thomas Banks, was a cheesemonger. Elected a King's Scholar at Eton in 1716 he was admitted a scholar at King's College, Cambridge, on October 6, 1720, was a fellow from 1723 to 1741, and proceeded to the degrees of B.A. (1724–5), M.A. (1728), and M.D. (1735). He held the chair of anatomy from 1735 to 1746; but, judging from his appointments and activities in London, he must have been much of an absentee. He was elected physician to Christ's Hospital in April 1737; at the Royal College of Physicians of London, of which he became a member on June 25, 1736, and a fellow on June 25, 1737, he was Goulstonian Lecturer in 1738, Censor in 1739, and Harveian Orator in 1743. His only published work seems to have been his Harveian Oration. His death in November 1746 was ascribed to sleeping in a damp bed.

REFERENCE

Roll Roy. Coll. Physicians of London, by W. MUNK, II, 134, London, 1878.

WILLIAM GIBSON (1714–1753), M.D.
Professor of Anatomy 1746–1753

William Gibson, who was born at Stead Hall, Halifax, Yorks, was admitted a sizar at Jesus College on December 17, 1731, and a scholar in 1736. He proceeded to the degrees of B.A. (1739) and M.D. (1746), and on December 5, 1746, after a contested election with Samuel Hutchinson, fellow of St John's, and John Scotman, fellow of Caius, became Professor of Anatomy. As he practised at Brigham in Yorkshire he also must have been an absentee, for he held the chair until his death on February 16, 1753.

Charles Collignon was the son of Paul Collignon of London but of French extraction. Admitted a pensioner of Trinity in 1743, he was re-admitted as a fellow-commoner on May 18, 1748, and graduated as M.B. in 1749, proceeding M.D. in 1754. He practised medicine in Cambridge, and was physician to Addenbrooke's Hospital from 1766 until his death. Appointed to the chair of anatomy in 1753, he taught and gave a course of twenty-eight lectures in the Lent term only. A grim incident occurred in 1768, when a body in the dissecting room, bought from London "resurrectionists", was recognized as that of Laurence Sterne (1713–1768) of Jesus, who died of pulmonary tuberculosis on March 18 in Old Bond Street, was buried on March 22 in St George's burial ground in the Bayswater Road, and removed two days later. His skeleton was preserved at Cambridge, but Macalister was unable to identify his skull with certainty. Dr W. L. H. Duckworth writes:

The collection, however, contains a skull labelled in Macalister's handwriting "Collignon Collection". To assign this to Laurence Sterne's skeleton is tempting, but no direct evidence has so far come to light. The existence of an old fracture of the right nasal bone, possibly the result of an accident in infancy through the fall of a window sash, might possibly provide a means of identification which as yet cannot be claimed.

In 1770 William Cole described Collignon as the most suitable person possible for his professorial duties "as he is a perfect skeleton himself, absolutely a walking skeleton, nothing but skin and bone". On May 3, 1770, he was elected a fellow of the Royal Society, and wrote a number of books chiefly "in the nature of moral reflections based on a little anatomy and medicine", for example *An Enquiry into the Structure of the human Body relative to its supposed Influence on the Morals of Mankind*, 8vo, Cambridge, 1764. In 1786 his collected works were published. His only daughter Catherine (1755–1832), who translated Abbé Ladvocat's *Historical and Biographical Dictionary* in 4 volumes, 1792, is, like her father, noticed in the *Dictionary of National Biography*. He died on October 1, 1785, and was succeeded by Sir Busick Harwood (*vide* p. 201).

REFERENCES

BETTANY, G. T. *Dictionary of National Biography*, IV, 811, London, 1908.
MACALISTER, A. *The History of the Study of Anatomy at Cambridge*, 1891.

After Busick Harwood's death there was a sharply contested election for the chair on November 23, 1814, which resulted as follows: John Haviland, M.A., St John's (*vide* p. 167), 150 votes, William Clark, M.A., fellow of Trinity, 135 votes, and John Thomas Woodhouse, M.D., Caius, physician to Addenbrooke's Hospital (1814–1828), 60 votes. The election was noteworthy for the appearance of Lord Byron, who came up to vote for Clark and was cheered by the undergraduates in the Senate House. When Haviland resigned the chair on becoming Regius Professor of Physic in 1817 Clark and Woodhouse were again candidates, but as the latter retired before the day of election Clark was elected without opposition.

WILLIAM CLARK (1788–1869), M.D., F.R.S.

Professor of Anatomy 1817–1865

William Clark was the second son of John Clark (1744–1805), M.D., founder of the Newcastle-on-Tyne Infirmary, and was born at Newcastle-on-Tyne on April 5, 1788. Entering Trinity College in October, 1804, he became a scholar in 1807, and being seventh wrangler in 1808 was elected a fellow in the following year. He then started medicine under John Abernethy (1764–1831) in London, and in 1813 obtained the licence to practise (M.L.), but did not proceed to the degree of M.D. until 1827. In 1817 he was elected Professor of Anatomy and in the following year took holy orders and travelled abroad with Sir M. M. Sykes for two years; he then took the opportunity of studying museums and obtained for use in Cambridge wax models of human anatomy from Calanzuoli of Bologna. The value of a museum was thus impressed on his mind and he did a great work in establishing the museum of comparative anatomy, generously helping it financially, and being influential in obtaining the collections of Brookes's Museum (1830) and Macartney (1836). He was elected a fellow of the Royal Society in 1836, but published little except a translation in 1856–8 of van der Hoeven's *Handbook of Zoology* in two volumes, for which

63

he learnt Dutch when over sixty years of age. The catalogue of the osteological portion of the specimens in the anatomical museum at Cambridge was brought out by him in 1862. Shipley spoke of him as "one of the founders of the School of Biology at Cambridge". Taking orders in 1818, he successively held the small livings of Arrington in Cambridgeshire, Wymeswold in Leicestershire, and the valuable rectory of Guiseley near Leeds (1826), but on this account was never away from Cambridge more than three months during the year. When the Natural Sciences Tripos was established in 1848 (the first examination being in 1851) he handed over the teaching of human anatomy and physiology to G. M. Humphry, and finally resigned his chair in November 1865. He had long advocated, especially before the Royal Commission in 1852, the establishment of two chairs, one of comparative, the other of human anatomy. A Syndicate appointed on May 11, 1865, to consider the best means of providing for the teaching of anatomy and zoology, reported in June, and recommended the creation of an additional professorship of zoology and comparative anatomy. This was done, and in 1866 the two chairs were filled; Alfred Newton (1829–1907), late fellow of Magdalene, after a contest (110 to 82 votes) with W. H. Drosier (1814–1889), M.D., of Gonville and Caius College, who as deputy had lectured on the subject since 1860, was elected into the zoological chair, and Humphry into that of anatomy, the only suggestion of opposition to his election being an application by C. Lesturgeon, surgeon to Addenbrooke's Hospital, who retired before the election.

William Clark was colloquially known as "Bone" Clark to distinguish him from "Stone" Clarke (Edward Daniel Clarke (1769–1822), the traveller, Professor of Mineralogy 1808–1822), and "Tone" Clarke (John Clarke, afterwards Clarke-Whitfeld (1770–1836), Professor of Music 1821–1836).

He married in 1827 Mary, daughter of Robert Darling Willis (1760–1821), M.D., F.R.C.P., of Gonville and Caius College, who attended George III in his fourth attack of mental disturbance in 1810, and was the member of the Willis family mentioned with Matthew Baillie (1761–1823) and William Heberden the younger (1767–1845) in the lines:

> The King employs three Doctors daily—
> Willis, Heberden and Baillie,
> All extremely clever men—
> Baillie, Willis, Heberden,
> But doubtful which most sure to kill is—
> Baillie, Heberden, or Willis.

Clark and his wife first lived at 17 Trumpington Street, where John Haviland, P. W. Latham, and H. B. Roderick followed them; in the drawing room of this house their only surviving son was born, John Willis Clark (1833–1910), the Superintendent of the Museum of Comparative Anatomy (1866–1891) and Registrary of the University (1891–1910). Clark had a paralytic stroke in 1863, rapidly aged afterwards, and died on September 15, 1869, in Scroope House which he had built in 1837–8, opposite to 17 Trumpington Street. The Scroope House site was purchased by the University in 1919 and is now occupied by the Engineering School and laboratories. A testi-

monial, got up in 1866, resulted in the execution of his
bust, which is in the Museum of Comparative Anatomy.

REFERENCES

Dictionary of National Biography, x, 409, London, 1887.
SHIPLEY, A. E. "*J.*" *A Memoir of John Willis Clark*, London, 1913.

SIR GEORGE MURRAY HUMPHRY (1820–1896), M.D., F.R.S.

Professor of Anatomy 1866–1883
Professor of Surgery 1883–1896

George Murray Humphry was born on July 18, 1820, at
Sudbury in Suffolk, the freedom of which he received in
1892, as the third son of William Wood Humphry,
barrister-at-law and distributor of stamps for Suffolk.
His elder brother, William Gilson Humphry (1815–1880)
was senior classic (1837), fellow of Trinity, vicar of St
Martin's-in-the-Fields, and author of many works including a *Commentary on the Acts of the Apostles* (1847).
After education at the local Grammar Schools of Sudbury
and Dedham, he was on account of *res angusta domi* at the
age of sixteen apprenticed to John Green Crosse (1790–
1850), a favourite pupil of James Macartney, Professor of
Anatomy in Trinity College, Dublin, in the year that this
well known lithotomist (Crosse) was elected a fellow of the
Royal Society; adjoining Crosse's surgery was a museum
and library in which Humphry became imbued with the
value of a museum. At the same time he worked as a
dresser in the Norfolk and Norwich Hospital. This early

start in professional work he evidently realized as a handicap, for in his Hunterian Oration at the Royal College of Surgeons of England in 1879 he said that twenty—John Hunter's age when he began medical work—was the best time to begin, and that the medical profession had suffered in quality, status, and practical outcome from having often been commenced too early in life; it may have been more than a coincidence that although he took the M.B. degree at Cambridge in 1852 he did not proceed to the M.D. until 1859, after the obligation to write the thesis in Latin had been removed.

Entering the Medical School of St Bartholomew's Hospital, London, in 1839, he came under the influence of Peter Mere Latham (1789–1875), William Lawrence (1783–1867) and James Paget (1813–1899), then curator of the museum, and he almost certainly modelled his teaching on the emphatic example of Latham. In 1840 he obtained the gold medal for anatomy and physiology in the first M.B. examination at the University of London, but never proceeded to the final examination; on November 19, 1841, he was admitted a member of the Royal College of Surgeons of England, and on May 12, 1842, became a licentiate of the Society of Apothecaries of London. On October 31, 1842, he was with the recommendation of George and James Paget elected surgeon to Addenbrooke's Hospital, thus becoming in his twenty-second year the youngest hospital surgeon in Great Britain, and held the post until 1894, a period of fifty-two years. In December of the same year as his election, the medical staff obtained permission from the Hospital Board to give clinical lectures, which Humphry at once proceeded to do. When in 1844 the new order of fellows at the Royal College of Surgeons of England was founded, he was, in virtue of his hospital appointment, elected a fellow on August 26 and being then a year under the statutory age his name appeared last on the list. In 1847 he entered the University by becoming a fellow-commoner of Downing, of which College he was elected an honorary fellow in 1869, and proceeded to the degrees of M.B. (1852) and M.D. (1859); in his thesis for the latter "On the formation of clots in the venous system during life" he drew on his own three attacks of phlebitis. After becoming responsible about 1848 for the teaching of human anatomy at the request of Professor William Clark, he had considerable difficulty in obtaining subjects for dissection, but was ably seconded by one Sims, whose efficiency Humphry summed up by describing him as "the most truthful liar he had ever known". In 1849 he gave a series of twenty-eight lectures on surgery which were published in the *Provincial Medical and Surgical Journal* (1849–50). His important *Treatise on the Human Skeleton, including the Joints,* with sixty illustrations drawn by his wife, came out in 1858, and was the outcome of many years' work. It was one of the earliest attempts to bring human anatomy into line with scientific morphology, made the dry bones live, was a source from which many lecturers extracted rich ore, and no doubt helped to secure his election as a fellow of the Royal Society in 1859. No second edition of this classic ever appeared, but what appears to be the manuscript intended for this purpose is preserved in the anatomical Department. It was followed by a constant stream of papers on anatomical, pathological, and surgical subjects.

Anxious to enable medical students of small means to come to the University, he established about 1860 "Dr Humphry's Hostel for Medical Students" at 56 Trumpington Street, which ceased in 1863. As a result of his energetic advocacy, Addenbrooke's Hospital was largely rebuilt in 1864–5 from plans he prepared.

In 1864 he was president of the surgical section at the Cambridge meeting of the British Medical Association, and in his address insisted on pathology, in all its branches, as the very cornerstone of surgery, and expressed regret that the Universities of Oxford and Cambridge had done so little for surgery. It may be mentioned that, much later, in speaking of Sir Henry Acland (1815–1900), Regius Professor of Medicine at Oxford (1858–1894), he said that Acland's work had been a stimulus to the establishment of the modern medical school at Cambridge. His ambition to promote a complete school of medicine (*vide* p. 27) in Cambridge was also shown in 1880, when the British Medical Association again met in that university town under his presidency. In his presidential address he discussed and partly explained why "Cambridge, more than any university in the world, with perhaps one exception, had banished medicine from its walls, and the men of medicine from its schools". He hoped that when next the Association came to Cambridge there would be a medical tripos. It was forty years on, in 1920, before the Association met there again, and it was not until 1925 that pathology became a subject in the second part of the Natural Sciences Tripos; the question of a Medical Tripos was much discussed in 1931. In his 1880 address he also advocated and subsequently organized a Collective

Investigation of Disease Committee, of which he became the chairman. An extensive scheme was at once set in being, with fifty-four committees, including 800 to 1000 of the chief practitioners in the kingdom. He edited the "Collective Investigation Records", the first in June 1883 with the assistance of F. A. Mahomed (1849–1884), and in 1889 brought out his book on "Old Age", in which he analysed the records of 824 persons between the ages of eighty and a hundred years, a very large number of whom he personally investigated. On this favourite subject he had been engaged for a considerable time, and in 1885 had utilized it for the annual oration at the Medical Society of London. A guide to Cambridge written by him for the meeting of the British Medical Association was afterwards expanded and went through several editions.

After teaching human anatomy for eighteen years he was elected the first professor of human anatomy in 1866, and in the same year with William Turner (1832–1916) of Edinburgh founded and edited the *Journal of Anatomy and Physiology* which contained a number of his papers on muscular homologies, published in book form in 1872. As mentioned elsewhere (*vide* p. 79) he made the first move towards the establishment of a physiological chair, and eventually Michael Foster was brought to Cambridge in 1870. Humphry lectured on physiology as well as on human anatomy. In order to strengthen the physiological side of the *Journal of Anatomy and Physiology* he obtained the co-operation of Michael Foster and William Rutherford (1839–1899) of Edinburgh on the editorial board from 1876 to 1878. But when the *Journal of Physiology* was started by Foster in 1878, papers on that subject were naturally addressed there in the first instance, and in 1916, after Turner's death, the title was abbreviated to the *Journal of Anatomy*, and the management and ownership passed into the hands of the Anatomical Society of Great Britain and Ireland which was founded in May 1887. As Humphry founded the *Journal of Anatomy and Physiology*, first published in Cambridge, and was active with C. B. Lockwood (1858–1914) in the establishment of the Anatomical Society of which he was the first president, there is a close similarity to Michael Foster's activity in the initiation of the *Journal of Physiology* and of the Physiological Society (*vide* p. 90).

At the Royal College of Surgeons of England he was on the Council from 1864 to 1884, a member of the Court of Examiners from 1877 to 1887, and gave the Arris and Gale lectures on anatomy and physiology in 1872 and 1873 in which he dealt with myology. In 1879 he delivered the Hunterian Oration, which corresponds to the Harveian Oration at the sister College of Physicians; in it he insisted on the philosophical outlook of John Hunter, with whom he was compared after his death by C. B. Lockwood. For the higher offices of president and vice-president he declined to be nominated as it would have interfered too greatly with his work at Cambridge. In 1869 he succeeded Sir George Paget, who then became president, as the representative of Cambridge on the General Medical Council, and held this post for twenty years. This experience increased the authority of his account in *The Student's Guide to the University of Cambridge* of "Degrees in Medicine and Surgery" which was reprinted in pamphlet form and reached a fifth edition in 1901.

"Man, Past, Present, and Future" formed the subject matter of his Sir Robert Rede lecture in 1880 before the University of Cambridge. Out of the seventy-two lecturers from 1859 to 1930 inclusive he is the only surgeon, and except for Norman Moore, who in 1915 lectured on "St Bartholomew's Hospital in Peace and War", the only medical man in practice to be thus honoured. Richard Owen, Huxley, Michael Foster, and W. A. Miller (1817–1870) the chemist are the other lecturers with medical qualifications.

In the early 'eighties of the last century the emoluments of the chair of human anatomy, which at first had hardly met expenses, became substantial from the fees of the now populous Medical School, and accordingly in 1883, after teaching it for 36 years, Humphry made way for a whole-time human anatomist, Macalister, and undertook without any stipend the professorship of surgery then founded by the University. His letter of January 22, 1883, resigning the anatomical chair and mentioning that he was willing to take the surgical chair without stipend is preserved in the University Registry. He was fond of maintaining the optimistic doctrine that the efficiency of a teacher increases as his salary falls, and that the usefulness of a University is enhanced by every decline in its revenue. He paid the salary of the assistant (Joseph Griffiths) to the Professor of Surgery appointed by Grace of May 1888.

As a surgeon he was skilful, resourceful, and successful; qualified long before the introduction of anaesthesia and antiseptics, he sometimes dispensed with an anaesthetic, and never followed the antiseptic routine, treating wounds by what he called the open method—by covering them

PROFESSOR SIR GEORGE MURRAY HUMPHRY
M.D., F.R.S.

with a piece of gauze. His papers on excision of the knee-joint had a powerful influence in establishing this operation, even in pre-Listerian days, and his hospital patients, rather afraid of his enthusiasm, were known to say "Now, Dr Humphry, I am not going to have my knee took out". His papers on surgery and pathology covered a wide field of subjects, such as vesical tumours and calculi, diseases of the male organs of generation, senile hypertrophy and senile atrophy of the skull, macrodactyly, and tetanus in addition to those already mentioned. After the death of William Whewell (1794–1866), Master of Trinity, Humphry is reported to have said that from an examination of his brain, which weighed only 49 oz., he would, had he not met with the fatal accident, have had a stroke within five months (R. Gower).

He was a magnetic teacher, employed the Socratic method and, keen observer himself, urged this attitude on his pupils. In lecturing and teaching he laid much stress on function, so that his anatomical instruction was familiarly known as "Humphryology" and thought to be of little use for examinations except his own, but their value in later clinical work soon became obvious. Of few clinical teachers were so many aphorisms quoted; a frequent and favourite injunction ran: "Eyes first and much, hands next and least, tongue not at all". On one occasion a student not remarkable for ability somewhat unexpectedly answered a question correctly, and followed it up by the unwise comment "You seem surprised, Professor", only to be discomfited by the prompt retort "So was Balaam when his ass spoke". To an incautious barrister in court, who asked if he was accustomed to lose many of his patients, he replied that he did not conduct his surgical cases as the cross-examiner did his legal cases, "otherwise he would lose them all".

With a keen interest in morbid anatomy he was an indefatigable collector of specimens for the museum, and he was appropriately president of the old Pathological Society of London 1891–3. He was knighted in January 1891, was a professorial fellow of King's College, Cambridge (1884), and received the honorary degrees of LL.D. Edinburgh (1891) and D.Sc. Dublin (1892). He was a corresponding member of the Paris Surgical Society, and in 1892 succeeded George Paget as president of the Cambridge Graduates' Medical Club which was established in 1883.

After a long illness he died at his house, Grove Lodge, Cambridge, on September 24, 1896, and was buried in the Mill Road Cemetery on September 29. His portrait by W. W. Ouless is in the Fitzwilliam Museum, and one by Miss K. M. Humphry in the surgical department of the Medical School. His bust by Wiles was presented to Addenbrooke's Hospital in May 1891. Another bust was executed by H. R. Hope-Pinker, R.A.

REFERENCES

ALLEN, F. J. *Brit. Med. Journ.* 1920, i, 651.
GOWER, RONALD. *Reminiscences*, p. 151, 1895.
Lancet, 1896, ii, 964–8.
LOCKWOOD, C. B. "In Memoriam Sir G. M. Humphry," *St. Bartholomew's Hosp. Rep.* 1897, XXXII, xxxi–xxxvii.
PLARR'S *Lives of the Fellows of the Royal College of Surgeons of England*, I, 581–4, Bristol and London, 1930.

ALEXANDER MACALISTER (1844–1919),

M.D., F.R.S.

Professor of Anatomy 1883–1919

Alexander Macalister was born in Dublin on April 9, 1844, and was the second son of Robert Macalister who had migrated from Paisley to succeed William Carleton (1794–1869), the Irish novelist, as secretary of the Sunday School Society. Coming of a large and needy family, Alexander was destined for a business career, but early in life displaying a love for biology he was allowed by special concession to begin medical work at the Royal College of Surgeons of Ireland at the tender age of fourteen years, and became a demonstrator of anatomy at sixteen, doubly qualified at seventeen, and lecturer in zoology in the University of Dublin in 1869; as he had entered Trinity College in 1867 he was still an under-graduate and had the peculiar experience of finding him-self debarred from entering for an honours' degree in zoology as he would have been *ex officio* his own examiner. On December 9, 1871, this post was changed to a pro-fessorial chair, and he became Professor of Comparative Anatomy and held this chair until 1883. On October 14, 1879, he was elected Professor of Anatomy and Chirurgery in Trinity College, Dublin, and Surgeon to Sir Patrick Dun's Hospital, with the proviso that he should not undertake private practice. On October 15, 1881, Mac-alister was "relieved from duty" at Sir Patrick Dun's Hospital. When he was twenty-six years of age he had taken part in the dissection of 639 subjects. On June 2, 1881, he was elected a fellow of the Royal Society. In

1883 he succeeded Humphry as Professor of Anatomy, and was elected a professorial fellow of St John's College, Cambridge. He held the chair for thirty-six years, the same period that William Turner (1832–1916) was Professor of Anatomy (1867–1903) at Edinburgh. The conditions at Cambridge led to a change in his activities; he became less concerned with myology than he had been in Dublin, where his association with Samuel Haughton (1821–1897) and the facilities of the Zoological Gardens had influenced this line of investigation in a rather special manner. Cambridge provided him with greater opportunities than he had enjoyed previously for the cultivation of his hobbies, archaeology, Egyptian philology, and theology. He kept up, however, an accurate record of abnormalities, which might have formed a continuation of his "Observation of Muscular Anomalies" read in abstract before the Royal Irish Academy in 1871. He had the most extensive knowledge of anatomy and wrote much, especially in his earlier years, his most remarkable works being an *Introduction to Animal Morphology* (1876), *Morphology of Vertebrate Animals* (1878), and *Textbook of Human Anatomy* (1889). He took a very broad view of human anatomy, and included embryology, histology, and anthropology in his teaching. His *Textbook of Human Anatomy* included microscopical anatomy, which was taught in Cambridge in the practical work of Michael Foster's physiological course. Alex Hill (1856–1929), however, who was demonstrator (1882–8) and University lecturer (1888–1907) on anatomy, gave a course of practical histology during the Long Vacation for many years during Macalister's occupation of the chair.

PROFESSOR ALEXANDER MACALISTER, M.D., F.R.S.

William Sharpey (1802–1880) of University College, London, where Foster had been trained, introduced microscopical anatomy into the practical teaching of physiology, and Macalister in his textbook was one of the earliest to act on the principle, which he ascribed to Macartney, that anatomy deals with structure macroscopical and microscopical. An interleaved copy of his textbook was continually added to, and after a few years overflowed with new information and observations; its disappearance, though philosophically borne, was a severe blow and explains why no second edition ever appeared. His knowledge of the history of anatomy was unrivalled, and in the Easter terms he often gave a short course of lectures on the subject, both systematic and on other aspects, such as "Eponymous Structures in Human Anatomy" (1889); but, though "A Sketch of the History of Anatomy in Ireland" (1884), the "Memoir of James Macartney" (1900), "The History of the Study of Anatomy in Cambridge" (1901), "Some Pioneer Medical Books" (1904), and his "Archaeologia Anatomica" in the *Journal of Anatomy and Physiology*, of which he was the chief acting editor from 1897 to 1917, gave forecasts of what he could have done, he never brought out "the detailed history of the progress of anatomical study" referred to in his introduction to his *Textbook of Human Anatomy*. Professor E. Barclay-Smith, his pupil and demonstrator, wrote that he "elevated anatomy from a mechanical study into a living science". In addition he was an able mathematician, a linguist, and an authority on archaeology, anthropology, theology, Biblical history, and Egyptology. His writings, numerous and on many

77

subjects, give no real idea of his knowledge and learning. The triumvirate of Paget, Humphry, and Michael Foster laid the firm foundations of the success of the Medical School, and Macalister's share in building thereon has not been sufficiently realized.

With a fine constitution he was a great walker, and accomplished the journey from Cambridge to London in little more than twelve hours. "A world-wide traveller, sea-voyages had no terrors for him, and he had the priceless gift of feeling as comfortable in a small tramp steamer as on the largest liner. Naturally imperturbable, he could rise superior even to the restraints of quarantine in an open Turkish sea-port ('I took the opportunity of acquiring the art of sail-making', he said)" (Duckworth). According to one who knew him well, the dominating influences in his life were "devotion to religion and the accumulation of a knowledge of isolated facts".

After a long illness he died on September 2, 1919, at his house, Torrisdale, Lady Margaret Road, Cambridge.

REFERENCES

Barclay-Smith, E. "In Memoriam Professor A. Macalister," *Journ. Anat.* Cambridge, 1919, LIV, 96.
Duckworth, W. L. H. *Man*, London, 1919, XIX, 164.

III. *Department of Physiology*

AS mentioned elsewhere (*vide* p. 17) the first physiological laboratory in Cambridge may be regarded as that provided by Richard Bentley (1662–1742), Master of Trinity, in what is now the bursary of the college. Here Stephen Hales (1677–1761) first measured blood-pressure and worked at animal and plant physiology in the early years of the eighteenth century. It was not, however, until the last third of the nineteenth century that experimental as distinguished from theoretical physiology found a permanent home in Cambridge. This came about in the following way: recognizing the need, Humphry, who lectured on physiology as well as human anatomy, advocated the establishment of a chair of physiology, but difficulties caused delay; later with the backing of George Eliot (Mary Ann Cross, 1819–1880), George Henry Lewes (1817–1878), and two influential fellows of Trinity, Coutts Trotter (1837–1887) and W. G. Clark (1821–1878), that college was persuaded to create the post of praelector in physiology who should teach the undergraduates of the University as a whole. To this post, which carried a fellowship, Michael Foster was appointed in 1870 on Huxley's recommendation, and brought from University College as his demonstrator Henry Newell Martin (1849–1896), who in 1876 became the first professor of physiology

79

at the Johns Hopkins University, Baltimore. Grace of June 23, 1870, "gave leave to Mr Michael Foster recently elected Praelector in Physiology in Trinity College to give lectures in physiology in one of the rooms in the New Museums Building". This room, then intended for a museum of philosophical instruments and now the Philosophical Library, was provided by the University and equipped by Trinity College; it served as a lecture room and laboratory for physiology, elementary biology, and embryology. Beginning in this small way and under considerable difficulties, Foster steadily laid the foundations of a great school.

After much discussion dating from 1872, a physiological department was built and occupied in January 1879, and was much enlarged in 1887 and again in 1890. But with the increasing number of students and the urgent need for rooms for research work in various directions it became quite inadequate. On November 10, 1910, the generous offer of the Drapers' Company of London to erect a new physiological department at a cost not exceeding £22,000 and £1000 for equipment was accepted; Sir Thomas Jackson, R.A., was the architect, and a building of five stories, connected on one side at right angles with the Department of Psychology opened in the previous year, was presented to the University and opened by Prince Arthur of Connaught on June 9, 1914. This building was from the first planned with a view to a later extension northwards and to include a large lecture room. In a Report dated April 28, 1931, the Buildings Syndicate recommended this extension in the form of a wing northwards up to a line in continuation of the south wall of the

Botany School, funds having become available from the Rockefeller Benefaction.

With great power of organization and of inspiring enthusiasm for biology Foster attracted students, some of the most distinguished of whom, such as F. M. Balfour (1851–1882), W. H. Gaskell, who was a wrangler, J. N. Langley, and A. Sheridan Lea (1853–1915), who originally was interested in classics, had not any previous leanings to science. Thus he initiated schools of research not only in animal physiology but in other branches of biology: embryology (F. M. Balfour) and plant physiology (S. H. Vines, Francis Darwin). He originated the practical courses in physiology now universal, and at first lectured on embryology and elementary biology as well as physiology; he very soon handed over the teaching of embryology to F. M. Balfour, and in 1882 transferred that of elementary biology to Adam Sedgwick (1854–1913) and S. H. Vines. After the report of the Royal Commission (appointed in 1877) the professorship of Physiology was established by Grace of May 10, 1883, and on June 11 Foster was appointed, with a stipend of £800 subject to a deduction of £200 if the professor, who was not allowed to undertake private practice, was the Master or a fellow of a college. Since 1920 the stipend has been £1200.

Founded by Foster, the Cambridge school of physiology developed with the assistance of his pupils Walter Holbrook Gaskell, the man of great conceptions, John Newport Langley, whose patient work for fifty-two years was of such a character that his results have remained unshaken, and Sheridan Lea. Among his numerous influential pupils were C. S. Sherrington, W. B. Hardy,

H. K. Anderson, J. Barcroft, and H. H. Dale. Foster brought W. H. R. Rivers in 1893 and Gowland Hopkins in 1898 to Cambridge, and thus introduced the moving spirits in the establishment of the Experimental Psychology and Biochemical Departments which therefore developed as offshoots from the Physiological Department. After Foster's time Cambridge physiologists, such as A. V. Hill and E. D. Adrian, both Foulerton Research Fellows, Keith Lucas (1879–1916) and G. R. Mines (1885–1914), both prematurely cut off, and others carried on the tradition.

The Journal of Physiology was founded by Michael Foster in 1878 with the financial assistance of his pupil A. G. Dew-Smith (1848–1903), who in 1881 founded the Cambridge Scientific Instrument Company, now the Cambridge Instrument Company Ltd. The journal was in some degree the successor of *Studies from the Physiological Laboratory in the University of Cambridge*, of which three parts appeared in 1873, 1876, and 1877, "edited by the Trinity Praelector in Physiology" and bearing the arms of that college on the grey covers. The expenses of the journal were such that in 1894 it was in danger of becoming bankrupt; Langley then took over the editorship and financial responsibility, with a subsidy from the Physiological Society. After his death in 1925 it became the property of the Physiological Society and was edited by a committee under the chairmanship of C. S. Sherrington.

The University teaching posts in the Department are the professor, three lecturers, and one demonstrator. The routine teaching is largely carried out by junior teachers appointed from year to year by the head of the Department.

A Readership in Physiology, established from January 1, 1919, became vacant when Joseph Barcroft was elected Professor of Physiology in 1925. The Readership was still vacant when the New Statutes came into operation in 1926 and therefore lapsed under Statute D, XVI, 2.

Three Lectureships in Physiology were established by Grace, December 6, 1883 (*vide* p. 26); two of these are assigned to advanced physiology.

A Lectureship on the Physiology of the Senses, established by Grace, November 7, 1907, was vacated by the last holder in 1927, and there is not now a lecturer with this title.

Demonstrators in Physiology. As mentioned elsewhere (p. 79), Michael Foster when appointed Praelector in Physiology at Trinity College brought with him a demonstrator. By Grace of December 6, 1883, a senior demonstrator with a stipend of £200 and a junior demonstrator, towards whose stipend the University contributed £50 a year, were established. An additional demonstrator under the authority of a Grace of December 1890, and a second additional demonstrator under the authority of a Grace of May 23, 1907, were appointed. At present (1931) there is only one University demonstrator, the routine teaching in the practical classes being largely carried out by junior teachers appointed from year to year by the Head of the Department.

The Michael Foster Studentship for encouragement of research in physiology, endowed by Jamieson Boyd Hurry (1857–1930), M.D. of St John's College, was accepted by Grace 2 of March 1912. It is of the value of £105 a year; the student shall carry on research in Cambridge unless the electors grant permission to work elsewhere.

The Gedge Prize for original observations in any branch of physiology was founded by Joseph Gedge, M.B., in 1869, and is awarded every second year; the value is about £43.

Rolleston Memorial Prize founded in 1883 by public subscription at the University of Oxford in memory of George Rolleston

(1829–1881), Linacre Professor of Anatomy and Physiology, is open to members of Cambridge as well as of Oxford University. It is awarded once in two years for original research in animal and vegetable morphology, physiology and pathology, and anthropology. The value is about £80.

The George Henry Lewes Studentship was founded in 1879 by "George Eliot" (Mary Ann Evans) "to advance the study of physiology by supplying students of either sex with the means of pursuing original investigations during the interval between their noviciate and their attaining the status of Professor". The capital sum of £5000 provided an annual income of £250 for the student who might hold it for one, two, three or in exceptional instances more years, but must devote his or her whole time to the work. The trustees appoint as director a physiologist of established reputation who is in charge of a physiological laboratory in Great Britain. So far the director has always been the Professor of Physiology at Cambridge. The following are the names of the early students with the dates of their appointment: C. S. Roy (1879), L. C. Wooldridge (1882), C. S. Sherrington (1884), J. Rose Bradford (1888), G. N. Stewart and E. H. Hankin (1889), J. S. Edkins (1892), J. W. Pickering (1894), H. M. Vernon and J. B. Leathes (1897), A. C. Hill (1899), H. H. Dale (1901), T. R. Elliott (1904), J. Mellanby (1907), A. V. Hill (1911), and A. N. Drury (1915).

REFERENCES

Historical Register of the University of Cambridge to the year 1910, edited by J. R. TANNER, pp. 247–52, Cambridge, 1917.

LANGLEY, J. N. *Methods and Problems of Medical Education* (Third Series), pp. 7–17, Rockefeller Foundation, New York, 1925.

PROFESSORS OF PHYSIOLOGY

	Appointed
Sir Michael Foster	1883
John Newport Langley	1903
Joseph Barcroft	1925

SIR MICHAEL FOSTER (1836–1907),

K.C.B., M.D., F.R.S.

Professor of Physiology 1883–1903

Michael Foster, born at Huntingdon on March 8, 1836, was the eldest of the ten children of Michael Foster (1810–1880), F.R.C.S., surgeon in that town, and Mercy Cooper. Educated until the age of thirteen years at the local Grammar School, he then went to University College School (1849–1852), and matriculating at London University in 1852 graduated B.A. with a University scholarship two years later. Had it not been for his non-conformist heritage he would have gone to Cambridge; as it was he followed his father's profession and, taking high honours in anatomy and physiology and in chemistry, graduated M.B. (1858) and M.D. (1859) at London University. After two years partly spent in medical study in Paris and at home and partly in original work, he was threatened with tuberculosis, and accordingly went as ship's surgeon in the *Union* chartered to build a lighthouse on the Asaruji rock opposite Mount Sinai on the Red Sea, but without any benefit. He then joined his father in general practice and his health improved; but, finding the life of a country doctor far from congenial, he gladly accepted an invitation in 1867 from his former teacher, William Sharpey, who was Professor of Anatomy and Physiology from 1836, the year of Foster's birth, until 1874, to inaugurate the teaching of practical physiology and histology at University College. In London he soon came under the influence of T. H. Huxley (1825–1895) whom he followed as Fullerian Professor of Physiology at the Royal Institution in 1869, a year after he was made Professor of Practical Physiology at University College. Like Ray Lankester (1847–1929), and William Rutherford (1839–1899), afterwards Professor of Physiology at Edinburgh, he assisted Huxley in his first class of elementary biology in 1870 at South Kensington.

In 1870, as already mentioned (*vide* p. 79), he was appointed Praelector of Physiology at Trinity College, and for the next thirty years the history of the birth and growth of the Cambridge school of physiology is inseparable from that of its father. His successor at University College, Sir John S. Burdon-Sanderson (1828–1905), was in 1882 appointed the first Waynflete Professor of Physiology at Oxford; so that the renaissance of physiology at the two older Universities was an offshoot from Sharpey's laboratory at University College, London. In 1872 Foster was elected a fellow of the Royal Society and one of the general secretaries of the British Association, a post he resigned four years later, though remaining actively interested in its proceedings. He collaborated with Burdon-Sanderson, Lauder Brunton, and E. E. Klein in a *Textbook for the Physiological Laboratory* (1873), and with his pupils F. M. Balfour in *The Elements of Embryology* (1874), and J. N. Langley in *A Course of Elementary Practical Physiology and Histology* (1876). His *Textbook of Physiology*, originally in one volume (1876), went through six editions, and part of a seventh with C. S. Sherrington in 1897, becoming divided into separate volumes, and was translated into German, Italian, and Russian. In response to congratulations, he warned his pupil J. G. Adami "Never write a textbook; if it is a failure it is time thrown away and worse than wasted; if it is a success, it is a millstone around your neck for the rest of your life". Adami, however, brought out the *Principles of Pathology* in two volumes, the first on general pathology (pp. 948) in 1909, and the second, jointly with A. G. Nicholls, on systemic pathology (pp. 1082) in 1910, which passed into a second edition in 1910 and 1911; a smaller *Textbook of Pathology* with John McCrae followed in 1912, with a second edition in 1914. In August 1880 Foster gave an address on Physiology at the Annual Meeting of the British Medical Association at Cambridge and insisted on the essential unity of physiology and pathology, asking the question what would be thought of the kindred science of meteorology if it were divided into two separate sciences dealing respectively with fine and bad weather? Huxley's *Scientific Memoirs* in four quarto volumes with a supplementary volume (1898–1903) were edited by Foster and Ray Lankester.

In 1881 Foster succeeded Huxley as biological secretary of the Royal Society and held the post for twenty-two years, thus surpassing the nineteen years' tenure of his teacher Sharpey. He was elected to the newly established chair of physiology in 1883. Following Humphry in 1880, he gave the Rede Lecture at Cambridge, taking "Weariness" as his subject in 1893. In 1899 he was President of the British Association at Dover, was created K.C.B. (Civil), thus recalling a previous knight, Sir Michael Foster (1689–1763), the just and childless judge, and brought out a life of Claude Bernard. Activities outside Cambridge continued to claim his co-operation; in 1900 he was elected Member of Parliament (Liberal-

PROFESSOR SIR MICHAEL FOSTER
K.C.B., M.D., F.R.S.

Unionist) for London University; he was chairman of the Royal Commission on Tuberculosis (1901–1906), and a member of the Royal Commissions on Vaccination (1889), on the Disposal of Sewage (1889), and on the Reorganization of the University of London. As a result of these demands on his time he applied for a deputy to perform his professional duties, and on March 25, 1900, Langley was appointed with a stipend of £300 a year, and Foster was given an emolument of the same amount for three years. In 1903 he resigned the chair and in 1906, having in the meanwhile crossed the floor of the House and joined the Liberal opposition, he lost his seat. His *History of Physiology* in the sixteenth, seventeenth and eighteenth centuries, the substance of his Lane Lectures at Cooper's College, San Francisco, in 1900, appeared in 1901, and was reprinted in 1924.

In addition to creating the Cambridge school of physiology and making physiology an aspect of biology instead of the younger sister of anatomy, he set the example of practical classes in physiology; the work in these classes included histology, a word introduced by Foster in consultation with F. B. Westcott (1825–1901) when Regius Professor of Divinity. As a lecturer his language was literary, concise, and critical; he used illustrations or diagrams little and the lantern never, being anxious to avoid anything that would distract attention from the spoken word. Foster the serious lecturer and Foster the witty after-dinner speaker were quite different personalities. The manuscript notes of his lectures are preserved in the Department. His charm and enthusiasm stimulated men to take up research as a noble life's work, and inspired them with an almost filial affection. Most successful as an organizer, he was the chief moving spirit in the establishment of the Physiological Society in 1876, the *Journal of Physiology* in 1878, of which he was the sole editor until 1894, and of the International Congress of Physiologists in 1889. As Secretary of the Royal Society he effected closer relations between the Government and the Society, and with such success that the Royal Society became expert adviser to many Government Departments as a matter of routine. He played an active part in initiating the International Association of Academies and in starting the *International Catalogue of Scientific Papers*. His original contributions to science were few and not important; "he was a discoverer of men rather than of facts" (Gaskell), and "worked for rather than at physiology". It is difficult to estimate how many undertakings and men's lives were determined and directed by his advice in his far-reaching spheres of influence. He received honorary degrees from Oxford, Glasgow, St Andrews, Dublin, and Montreal, and in 1891 was awarded the Baly Medal for distinction in physiology by the Royal College of Physicians of London. His portrait by Herkomer is in the possession of Trinity College, Cambridge.

He died suddenly in London on January 28, 1907, and was buried at Huntingdon.

REFERENCES

ADAMI, J. G. *Queen's Univ. Med. Faculty Publ.*, Kingston, Ont., No. 7, 1913.

ALLEN, F. J. *Brit. Med. Journ.*, 1920, i, 653.

GASKELL, W. H. *Proc. Roy. Soc.*, London, B, 1908, LXXX, lxxi.

LANGLEY, J. N. *Journ. Physiol.*, 1907, XXXV, 233; *Dictionary of National Biography*, Second Supplement, II, 44–46, London, 1912.

JOHN NEWPORT LANGLEY (1852–1925),

SC.D., F.R.S.

Professor of Physiology 1903–1925

John Newport Langley was born on November 10, 1852, at Newbury as the second son of John Langley, master of a private school, and Mary, eldest daughter of Richard Groom; he was educated at home and at Exeter Grammar School of which his uncle, the Rev. H. Newport, was head master. Entering St John's College, Cambridge, as a sizar in October 1871, he read mathematics and history until in his second year (May 1873) he became Foster's pupil. In 1874 he was elected a foundation scholar of the College and was placed second in order of merit, in a bracket of five, in the first class of the Natural Sciences Tripos which was then held in December. In the next year he succeeded Newell Martin as Foster's demonstrator and assisted Foster in writing *A Course of Practical Elementary Physiology and Histology*, 8vo (1876), which went through a number of editions, the seventh in 1899 being brought out by Langley and L. E. Shore. He continued to be demonstrator with the responsibility of the expanding laboratory and practical classes until in 1883 three University lectureships in physiology were established and occupied by W. H. Gaskell, A. Sheridan Lea, and himself. After a close contest with Sheridan Lea he was elected in 1877 to an open fellowship at Trinity. On March 25, 1900, he was appointed deputy professor with a stipend of £300 a year, half the amount that Foster received apart from a professional fellowship. Three years later on Foster's resignation he became professor of physiology, and thus gave the elementary lectures in that subject for a quarter of a century.

Langley's work was directed to solve two problems: for the first sixteen years he investigated secretory changes in glands, and for the remaining thirty-five years mainly the autonomic nervous system. Starting work as early as 1874, at Foster's suggestion, on the action of pilocarpine, this was followed by a series of papers on the histological changes that occur in resting and active secreting cells, showing, contrary to Heidenhain's view, that zymogen granules are stored in the cell during rest and disappear during activity. The results of years of research were summed up in his article on the salivary glands in Schäfer's *Textbook of Physiology*, 1898. Gaskell between 1886 and 1889 established the main facts about the autonomic system as it was subsequently called, and Langley's earlier work prepared him to investigate further the structure and functions of this portion of the nervous system. Beginning in 1890, a stream of about seventy papers, nineteen with Hugh K. Anderson (1865–1928), Master of Gonville and Caius (1912–1928), appeared on this subject, and in 1921 he brought out part I of *The Autonomic System*, which was translated into French and German. It can be said of few men that their

PROFESSOR J. N. LANGLEY, Sc.D., F.R.S.

work has never been upset, but so careful in his observations and so much on the look out for fallacies was Langley, that this verdict on his work has frequently been passed by his peers.

As editor of the *Journal of Physiology* from 1894 until his death, he did an enormous amount of critical and conscientious work, and, "unlike most editors, for him the acceptance of a paper meant often not the end, but the beginning of a task"; with a concise style he had an almost uncanny skill in condensing the papers of verbose contributors, and of clarifying tortuous arguments, this often resulting in his recasting or rewriting the paper. A really great editor, he changed the tradition of the physiological papers from that of the descriptive to that of the "exact" sciences (Hardy).

Although never allowing anything to interfere with his work, he had broad interests socially and in athletics; a runner in his youth, he played real and lawn tennis, rowed and sailed over the English rivers and fens, and was pre-eminent as a skater, being for a long period President of the University Skating Club. Like Foster and Gaskell, he was a keen gardener, and specially successful with tulips and roses.

Many honours rightly came to Langley; elected a fellow of the Royal Society on June 7, 1883, he received a Royal Medal in 1892, and was vice-president in 1904–5. In 1903 he was awarded the Baly Medal of the Royal College of Physicians of London for distinction in physiology, and in 1912 the Retzius Medal of the Swedish Society of Physicians. He was President of the Neurological Society of Great Britain in 1893, being the only one without a medical qualification. His honorary degrees included LL.D. St Andrews, Sc.D. Dublin, and M.D. Groningen, and a large number of foreign scientific societies made him an honorary or corresponding member.

He died on November 5, 1925, at his house, Hedgerley, Madingley Road, Cambridge, where he had lived since his marriage in 1902, having been in full work up to the onset of an attack of pneumonia.

REFERENCES

FLETCHER, W. M. *Proc. Roy. Soc.* B, 1927, CI, xxxiii–xli (with portrait); *Journ. Physiol.*, 1926, LXI, 1–27 (with portrait).
HARDY, W. B. *Brit. Med. Journ.*, 1925, ii, 924.

WALTER HOLBROOK GASKELL (1847–1914), M.D., F.R.S.

Walter Holbrook Gaskell was born on November 1, 1847, at Naples, where his father John Dakin Gaskell, a barrister, was spending the winter for reasons of health. His mother, Ann Gaskell, was his father's second cousin, and he was thus a second cousin once removed of Mrs Elizabeth Cleghorn Gaskell (née Stevenson, 1810–1865), the novelist. He was the third son, being the younger of twin sons. Living at Highgate, he was educated at Sir Roger Cholmeley's school, and entered Trinity College, Cambridge, on December 15, 1864, became a foundation scholar in 1868, and graduated B.A., being twenty-sixth

W. H. GASKELL, M.D., F.R.S.

wrangler in 1869. Then taking up medicine he became a pupil of Foster, and entered University College Hospital for clinical work in 1872; but in 1874 on Foster's advice he postponed his medical degree in order to work at Leipzig, then the chief centre of physiological research, under Carl Ludwig (1816–1895) on the nervous control of the circulation in the voluntary muscles of the frog. "This led him by a series of steps, which were perfectly logical, but impossible to foresee, from point to point of scientific enquiry up to his theory of the origin of vertebrates" (Langley). In 1875 he married Catherine Sharpe Parker, settled in Grantchester, and worked in Foster's laboratory on the vasomotor nerves of voluntary muscle, two papers on this subject appearing in the first volume of the *Journal of Physiology* in 1878. In this year he proceeded to the degree of M.D., but never engaged in medical practice. Then attacking the problem of the nerve supply and the causation of the contraction of the heart, he demonstrated the antagonistic action of the vagus and the cervical sympathetic, and eventually proved by a long series of experiments, chiefly on frogs and tortoises, that contraction arises in the heart muscle and is conducted by muscular continuity independently of the nerve ganglion-cells and fibres, the vagus and sympathetic system acting as regulators of this independent rhythm; he thus proved the correctness of the myogenic theory (1883). His observations on heart "block", a term adopted from Romanes' account of the passage of contraction waves in medusae, in connection with conduction from the auricle to the ventricle, were later confirmed by the string galvanometer. This work, the basis of modern conceptions of disordered mechanisms of the heart, was fully described in his article "The Contraction of Cardiac Muscle" in Schäfer's *Textbook of Physiology* (1900). From his study of the nerves of the heart he proceeded to investigate the structure, distribution, and function of the nerves of the visceral and vascular systems (1885 and 1886), thus establishing the present knowledge of the sympathetic nervous system, which Langley later extended in detail. Then taking up a problem of a more morphological character, he brought out in 1889 a paper on "The Relation between the Structure, Function, Distribution, and Origin of the Vertebrates"; his view that the vertebrates were descended from an arthropod stock represented by Limulus, the King crab, was supported by further papers with additional arguments, and roused vigorous opposition from biologists; but his book *The Origin of the Vertebrates* (1908) attracted little fresh attention. With L. E. Shore he undertook in 1890 an experimental research in connection with the Nizam of Hyderabad's Second Commission on the Cause of Death under Chloroform; they employed various methods, notably that of cross circulation from one animal to another; their results published in 1893 proved that chloroform acts directly on the heart, and that the fall of blood-pressure is not due to the action of chloroform on the vasomotor centre, thus controverting the Commission's conclusion that death is due to failure of the respiratory centre and that the pulse need not be regarded critically during anaesthesia so long as the respiration is carefully watched. This investigation was somewhat outside the scope of his other work. On September 3,

1914, he revised the last pages of a small book on the *Involuntary Nervous System*, published in 1916, and early the next morning had a cerebral haemorrhage, dying on September 7 at "The Uplands", Great Shelford, where he had lived since 1893.

Gaskell's work had wide bearings and is remarkable both for its accuracy and for the generalizations he based on it. He was elected a fellow of the Royal Society on June 8, 1882, fellow and praelector in natural science at Trinity Hall in 1889; he received the Marshall Hall Prize at the Royal Medical and Chirurgical Society in 1888, a Royal Medal from the Royal Society in 1889, and in 1895 the Baly Medal for distinction in physiology from the Royal College of Physicians of London. The Universities of Edinburgh and McGill conferred on him the honorary degree of LL.D.

REFERENCES

Information from J. F. Gaskell, M.D.
LANGLEY, J. N. *Proc. Roy. Soc.* B. 1915, LXXXVIII, xxvii.

IV. *Department of Biochemistry*

Sheridan Lea wrote the section on physiological chemistry in Foster's *Textbook of Physiology* and as University Lecturer on physiology from 1883 to 1896 dealt with that subject; this was carried on by A. Eichholz of Emmanuel College until a University lectureship in chemical physiology was established by Grace of June 12, 1898, and filled by the appointment of Frederick Gowland Hopkins, who in 1902 became Reader in that subject. In 1910 Trinity College added to this appointment a Praelectorship and a fellowship, and in 1914 the University elected him to the newly established professorship of biochemistry, tenable with the Readership and Praelectorship, but without any additional stipend. The Sir William Dunn Professorship of Biochemistry was established by Grace of February 12, 1921, and the previous chair of biochemistry was suppressed. This was endowed with £25,000 out of £165,000 conveyed to the University by the Trustees of the late Sir William Dunn.

The Department of Biochemistry was separately constituted in 1914; from 1908 the teaching was carried on in part of the old physiological laboratory, and after this was vacated by Professor Langley, the whole of the available accommodation was used for biochemistry and from 1919 to 1924 additional space was provided in the Balfour Laboratories in Downing Place. The Dunn Trustees' benefaction erected and maintained the new department in Tennis Court Road, which was opened on May 9, 1924, by Lord Balfour.

Biochemistry was approved as a separate subject in the Natural Sciences Tripos, Part II, by Grace of June 11, 1924, on the recommendation made on May 19 by the Special Boards for Physics and Chemistry and for Biology and Geology, and the names of candidates taking this subject appeared in the tripos list of the following year. The number of research workers in the Department in recent years has averaged thirty-five.

Sir William Dunn Reader in Biochemistry was authorized by Grace of December 19, 1922, with a total stipend not exceeding £850 per annum, or if the Reader holds a fellowship £650.

Two Lectureships in Biochemistry, each with a stipend of £300 per annum, payable from the Sir William Dunn endowment, together with £50 from the Common University Fund, were established in 1921. These payments no longer hold good, as they were altered in 1926.

A Senior Demonstrator in Biochemistry, with a stipend of £150 payable from the Medical Grant Fund, was appointed by Grace of March 1, 1919. These payments have now been placed on a different footing.

The Benn W. Levy Fund and Studentship, accepted by Grace of March 10, 1910, is devoted to the furtherance of original research in biochemistry. The value of the studentship is £100 a year, and it is open to members of the University of Cambridge who have been admitted to a degree, and to members of Girton and Newnham Colleges who have received the title of a degree.

V. *Department of Experimental Psychology*

THE history of the origin of experimental psychology in Cambridge is of interest, as it was originally so closely connected with the Department of Physiology. As long ago as 1877 James Ward (1843–1925), the first Professor of Mental Philosophy and Logic (1897–1925), and John Venn (1834–1923) put forward a proposal for a laboratory in psychophysics; had it not been successfully opposed on the plea that it was irreligious to put the human soul into a scale of quantities, Cambridge would have led the world in this respect. W. Wundt (1832–1920), who developed from being a physiologist into a psychologist, was in 1879 the first to organize a laboratory of experimental psychology in Leipzig. Ward obtained a University grant for psychological apparatus in 1891; in the same year Michael Foster set apart a room in his laboratory for psychological work on the special senses, and in October 1893 brought to Cambridge, as lecturer on the physiology of the sense organs, W. H. R. Rivers (1864–1922), who in 1897 was appointed University Lecturer in Physiological and Experimental Psychology. In November 1907 this lectureship was suppressed and two new ones substituted, (i) on the Physiology of the Senses, which Rivers held until 1916, and (ii) on Experimental Psychology, connected with the Special Board for Moral Science, which his pupil C. S. Myers, of Gonville and Caius College, held until January 1921, when he was made Reader in that subject. Rivers, who attained high distinction in clinical neurology, in the physiology of the senses, and in experimental psychology, later took an active part in ethnological investigations. A Department of Experimental Psychology, erected by funds largely supplied by the family of C. S. Myers, was opened in 1913. Myers, however, resigned in 1922, and was followed as Reader by F. C. Bartlett of St John's College, who in January 1931 became the first professor of experimental psychology. In 1922 a University lectureship in psychopathology was established, J. T. McCurdy, of Corpus Christi College, being appointed, and in 1931 a University demonstrator in experimental psychology was established from October 1, 1931.

The Pinsent-Darwin Fund and Studentship for original research into any problem which may have a bearing on mental defects, diseases, or disorders, was endowed in 1924 by the benefaction (£5000) of Mrs Pinsent and Sir Horace and the Hon. Lady Darwin. The studentship, tenable for three and not more than six years, is of the annual value of about £200. The student need not be a member of the University. The regulations for the studentship were approved by Grace of June 7, 1924.

VI. *Department of Pathology*

HAVILAND, when Regius Professor, gave lectures on general and special pathology, Bond followed this example, and Bradbury as Linacre Lecturer announced lectures on pathology and morbid anatomy from the Easter term of 1873 until 1884; but Humphry's impressive teaching of surgical pathology in connection with clinical practice was the most valuable until a whole-time chair of pathology was established by Grace of December 6, 1883, after having been under consideration for some years. In 1879 a memorial was addressed to the University Commissioners signed by 138 graduates of the University "engaged in the study or practice of medicine" praying that, in the new Statutes for the University, provision might be made for an extension of the study of medical science, especially of pathology, medicine, and surgery. The science of pathology, the memorialists continued, had, "in addition to its value as an essential part of the complete study of Medicine, now attained such precision, proportions, and development that it seems to us fairly to demand recognition as one of the foremost subjects in the sphere of University work."

The accommodation available for pathological work and teaching was very inadequate until 1904. C. S. Roy, the first professor, began with two small rooms on the third floor of Fawcett's building, over what was then the old Physiological Department, and lectured in the theatre of the old Anatomical School. During the academic years of 1885 and 1886 the numbers attending the classes were thirty-one and forty-six. In 1889 the Pathological Department moved into the old chemical laboratory which backed on Corn Exchange Street and was in a very dilapidated state, some of the structure dating back to 1786. When this refuge was pulled down in 1901 to provide part of the site for the new Medical School, the Pathological Department was temporarily accommodated in the premises in St Tibb's Row formerly occupied by the Cambridge Scientific Instrument Company. In 1904 the Pathological Department was organized by Sims Woodhead in the new Medical School which contained the Humphry Museum and the Kanthack Pathological Library. In 1924 the Trustees of the Rockefeller Foundation offered £100,000 to build a Pathological Department and £33,000 for its endowment contingent on the University raising £33,000. The late Ernest H. Gates's generous offer to provide the sum necessary to enable the University to accept the offer of the Rockefeller Trustees was approved by the University on October 18, 1924. This Pathological Department next to that of biochemistry in Tennis Court Road was planned by H. R. Dean (b. 1879), Professor of Pathology since 1922 and Master of Trinity Hall since 1929, who had previously been Professor of Pathology in the Universities of Sheffield and Manchester. The building, which houses the Humphry Museum and the Kanthack Pathological Library, and at first was shared by the Professor of Animal Pathology (J. B. Buxton), was completed in 1928.

As mentioned elsewhere (p. 38), the third part of the

second M.B. examination consists in elementary pharmacology, including pharmaceutical chemistry, and elementary general pathology and bacteriology. A short course in these subjects and elementary clinical work is provided twice a year, in the Lent term and Long vacation, as a brief introduction to the study of disease, for students who have passed the second part (human anatomy and physiology) of the second M.B. examination. Cambridge students are expected to do their clinical and applied pathology in the laboratories of the hospitals elsewhere, where they spend the three years of clinical study. Cambridge, however, presents unrivalled opportunities for the development of the study of pathology as abnormal biology in connection with the great schools of physiology, biochemistry, and other branches of biology. An important step in this direction was the inclusion of pathology as a subject in Part II of the Natural Sciences Tripos, approved by Grace of June 13, 1924, as a result of a recommendation made on May 19 of that year by the Special Boards for Physics and Chemistry and for Biology and Geology. This course in pathology, which occupies an academic year, started in the Michaelmas term, 1924, and the names of candidates taking it appeared in the tripos list of 1925. The development of pathology as an experimental science and as a branch of biology is important to both biology and medicine, and the new laboratories at Cambridge are well-equipped for the investigation of disease by experimental methods and for the training of research workers on these lines.

The stipend of the professor, who is not allowed to undertake private medical practice, was in 1883 fixed at

£800 per annum (or £600 if he holds a headship or fellowship of a college). Since 1920 the stipend has been £1200 with the same conditional reductions.

A Readership in Preventive Medicine. By Grace of February 10, 1923, this post was authorized with a stipend of £850 or, if the Reader holds a fellowship, £650. It is to terminate with the tenure of G. S. Graham-Smith, M.D., of Pembroke College, who was University Lecturer in Hygiene 1907–1923.

A Lectureship in Pathology was established by Grace of March 9, 1907. It was held until 1929 by Louis Cobbett, M.D., of Trinity, previously Professor of Pathology in the University of Sheffield (1906–7).

The Huddersfield Lectureship in Special Pathology was established by Grace of February 16, 1905, and was endowed at the instance of Professor Sir German Sims Woodhead by friends residing in or connected with Huddersfield. It was held by T. S. P. Strangeways (1866–1926) of St John's College until his death.

A Demonstratorship of Pathology was established by Grace of June 9, 1887. Among Roy's demonstrators, who afterwards were eminent pathologists, were Almroth Wright, J. G. Adami, and J. Lorrain Smith (1862–1931). In 1931 there were three demonstrators.

The John Lucas Walker Studentship and Exhibitions founded under the will of John Lucas Walker of Trinity College, who died in 1887, for original research in pathology, are open to either sex and the student need not necessarily be or become a member of the University. The place and nature of the student's studies are subject to the approval of the Professor of Pathology, provided that he shall work for at least three terms in Cambridge, unless the Professor of Pathology shall with the approval of the other Managers of the Fund dispense with this requirement for special reasons.

The Gwynaeth Pretty Research Fund and Studentship founded in memory of Miss Gwynaeth Pretty, accepted by Graces 2 of January 26 and 5 of March 1, 1929, are devoted to the encouragement of research in the etiology, pathology, or treatment of disease, with particular but not exclusive reference to those diseases which cripple or disable in childhood or early life. The income of the fund is entrusted to the professor of pathology and four other managers. The studentship may be awarded to persons of either sex whether members of the University or not, and is tenable for three years.

The Nita King Research Scholarship for the encouragement of original research in the etiology, pathology, and prevention of fevers was accepted by the Senate on December 17, 1917. It is of the annual value of £50, open to members of the University and students of Newnham or Girton, and tenable in the first instance for a period not exceeding three years. The conditions under which the research is to be conducted and the place or places in which it is to be carried on shall be determined by the Professor of Pathology in consultation with the other Managers.

PROFESSORS OF PATHOLOGY

	Appointed
Charles Smart Roy	1884
Alfredo Antunes Kanthack	1897
Sir German Sims Woodhead	1899
Henry Roy Dean	1922

CHARLES SMART ROY (1854-1897),

M.D., F.R.S.

Professor of Pathology 1884–1897

Charles Smart Roy was the seventh son of Adam Roy, shipowner, also a seventh son, and was born on January 27, 1854, at Arbroath in Forfarshire, the birth- and burial-place of William Sharpey (1802–1880), the physiologist. He was educated at St Andrews and medically at the University of Edinburgh, where he graduated M.B. in 1875 and was resident physician in the Royal Infirmary. Then, moving to London, he worked at the Animal Sanitary Institution in Wandsworth, founded by Thomas Brown who died in December 1852; but when war broke out in 1876 between Turkey and Serbia he joined the Turkish army as a surgeon. On his return he carried out research on pleuro-pneumonia at the Brown Institution before going to Berlin where he worked at pathology under Rudolf Virchow (1821–1902) and Robert Koch (1843–1910), and on the physiology of the heart with E. H. Du Bois-Reymond (1818–1896); for a time he was assistant to F. L. Goltz (1834–1902) in the physiological Institute at Strassburg, and later, after working with von Reckinghausen, investigated the pathology of the kidney at Leipzig in 1879 with Julius Cohnheim (1839–1884), who exerted a lasting influence upon him. His M.D. thesis on the factors which modify the work of the

PROFESSOR C. S. ROY
M.D., F.R.S.

heart was awarded a gold medal and half the Goodsir Memorial prize in 1878.

In 1879 he was elected the first George Henry Lewes Student in physiology, and while working in Foster's laboratory with the oncometer on the spleen and kidney lectured on advanced physiology. In 1881 he succeeded W. S. Greenfield (1846–1919) as Professor-Superintendent of the Brown Institution at Wandsworth, and during his term of office went to the Argentine to report on an outbreak of epizootic fever among cattle. On April 26, 1884, he was appointed the first Professor of Pathology at Cambridge, and in this same year was elected a fellow of the Royal Society on June 12, and a member of the Alpine Club. In the following year, together with C. S. Sherrington and J. J. Graham Brown (1853–1925) of Edinburgh, he went to Spain on a Commission appointed by the Royal Society to investigate the cholera epidemic. He was an expert experimentalist, a rapid and accurate operator, extremely successful in inventing instruments for taking graphic records, did pioneer work on the cardio-vascular system, showed the contractility of the capillaries in 1879 (with Graham Brown) and the rhythmic contractile power of the spleen (1882), and with Adami, who was his demonstrator (1888–1890), did a great deal of experimental work on the physiology and pathology of the mammalian heart. As a teacher he appealed more to the advanced student and those aiming at original research, to whom he was most helpful and generous, than to the ordinary pupil. He had many outside interests, being a great traveller, keen mountaineer, skilful sailor, and able linguist.

In 1892 he began to show signs of a nervous breakdown, and from the autumn of 1895 Kanthack acted as his deputy. He died on October 4, 1897, at 27 St Andrew's Street, Cambridge, and was buried in the Mill Road Cemetery.

REFERENCES

Brit. Med. Journ. 1897, ii, 1031, 1124.
Journ. Path. and Bacteriol. Edin. 1898, v, 143–6.
Lancet, 1897, ii, 954.

ALFREDO ANTUNES KANTHACK (1863-1898), M.D., F.R.C.P., F.R.C.S.

Professor of Pathology 1897–8

Alfredo Antunes Kanthack was born on March 4, 1863, at Bahia in Brazil, and was the son of Emilio Kanthack, British Consul at Pará, Brazil. After education at Hamburg and Luneburg, he came to England in 1881 and in 1882 worked at University College, Liverpool, taking the B.A. (1884), B.Sc. (1886), M.B. and B.S. (1888) of London University, all with honours, and eventually the M.D. (1892). In the honour list of the final M.B. he gained the gold medal in Obstetrics, and in Medicine was in the second class bracketed with E. H. Starling (1866–1927), just below J. Rose Bradford. Having in the meantime entered the Medical School of St Bartholomew's Hospital, London, in 1887, where he was a prominent member of the Rugby football team, he became a fellow of the Royal College of Surgeons of England on June 14, 1888; in 1889 he worked for a year under Virchow,

Yours ever
AAK.

PROFESSOR A. A. KANTHACK
M.D., F.R.C.P., F.R.C.S.

Koch, and Krause in Berlin. Returning to St Bartholomew's in the following year as obstetrical assistant to Matthews Duncan (1826–1890), he went with G. A. Buckmaster and B. Rake to India to investigate leprosy under the direction of the National Leprosy Fund. In 1891 he was elected John Lucas Walker Student in Pathology and, becoming a fellow-commoner at St John's College, Cambridge, worked in Roy's department on the wandering cells in frogs (1892), later (1894) supplemented by a similar investigation in mammals, on both occasions with W. B. Hardy, and on Madura foot. The two previous holders of the John Lucas Walker Studentship were William Hunter and J. G. Adami, and among the subsequent students were J. Lorrain Smith, L. Cobbett, J. W. W. Stephens, H. E. Durham, and G. S. Graham-Smith. In 1892 he returned to Liverpool as demonstrator of bacteriology and medical tutor with a view to practice. This, however, was cut short by his election in the same year as Director of the Pathological Department at St Bartholomew's Hospital, London, this being the first whole-time pathological appointment at a London Medical School. In addition he was curator of the museum and, as pathologist to the hospital, had the clinical material, previously dealt with in the wards, sent for examination in his department. His clear and enthusiastic teaching attracted many followers, among them T. S. P. Strangeways (1866–1926), who as demonstrator of pathology, later accompanied him to Cambridge. In the summer of 1894 he had a second and prolonged attack of typhoid fever and was treated in St Bartholomew's Hospital; but in spite of this illness he won the Jacksonian

Prize at the Royal College of Surgeons of England in 1895 with an essay on "The Aetiology of Tetanus and the Value of Serum Treatment". This annual prize of the value of twenty guineas was founded in 1800 by Samuel Jackson, F.R.S.

In the autumn of 1895 the state of Roy's health incapacitated him from carrying on the duties of the chair, and accordingly Kanthack became his deputy, combining this with his London duties and travelling to and fro. In 1897 he was elected a fellow of the Royal College of Physicians of London, moved to Cambridge, and after Roy's death in October was elected Professor of Pathology and a fellow of King's College. Unfortunately he held the chair for thirteen months only and died on December 21, 1898; after the funeral service in King's College Chapel on Christmas Eve, he was buried in the Histon Road Cemetery. Memorial Kanthack Libraries were established in the Pathological Departments of both St Bartholomew's Hospital and Cambridge. In his short life Kanthack did a surprising amount of work and stimulated a great deal in others; thus during the last ten years of his life he brought out seventy-four papers and books, twenty-eight of which were joint publications. Though he was part author of books on *Practical Morbid Anatomy* (with H. D. Rolleston, 1894) and *Practical Bacteriology* (with J. H. Drysdale, 1895), his most influential publication at the time was probably the article on "The General Pathology of Infection" in the first edition of Allbutt's *System of Medicine* (1896, 1, 503–86).

After Kanthack's death the obvious successor was J. G. Adami (1862–1926), and Allbutt and Foster warmly assured him of their support; but after some delay he felt bound for private reasons to remain in Montreal where he was Strathcona Professor of Pathology in McGill University from 1892 to 1915. The electors therefore chose German Sims Woodhead.

REFERENCES

Journ. Path. and Bacteriol. Edin. 1900, VI, 89.
Plarr's Lives of the Fellows of the Royal College of Surgeons of England, I, 641–3, London and Bristol, 1930.
St Bartholomew's Hosp. Journ. 1899, VI, 49–53 (with portrait, and bibliography of his publications by C. R. Hewitt).
St Bartholomew's Hosp. Rep. 1900, XXXV, 5–11. "In Memoriam," by A. A. B(owlby) (with portrait).

SIR GERMAN SIMS WOODHEAD (1855–1921),
K.B.E., M.D.
Professor of Pathology 1899–1921

German Sims Woodhead, who came of Quaker stock, was born on April 29, 1855, as the eldest son of Joseph Woodhead, editor and proprietor of the *Huddersfield Examiner* and at one time M.P. for the Spens Valley Division of Yorkshire. Educated at Huddersfield College, he began Medicine in 1873 at Edinburgh, where he was a prominent athlete in sprinting and Rugby football. For most of his life he was a keen volunteer, becoming Lieut.-Col., R.A.M.C. (T.F.), before the outbreak of the War. As an outstanding personality he was elected by his fellow-students to the Presidency of the Royal Medical Society, an office so often held by future leaders of the profession. Qualifying in 1878, he was both house-surgeon and house-physician in the Royal Infirmary, and after working in Vienna and Berlin returned to Edinburgh where he came under the influence of D. J. Hamilton (1849–1909), and proceeded to the degree of M.D. with a gold medal for a thesis on "Some Pathological Conditions in the Medulla Oblongata" in 1881. In the same year he became first assistant to W. S. Greenfield (1846–1919), who had just been elected to the chair of pathology, and subsequently pathologist to the Royal Infirmary and to the Royal Hospital for Sick Children, Edinburgh. In 1883 he brought out his *Practical Pathology*, which for thirty years was a standard textbook, and in 1885, with A. W. Hare, *Practical Mycology*, which was one of the first systematic books on bacteriology in English. He was the first exponent of the new science of bacteriology in Edinburgh, and in 1891 contributed to the Contemporary Science Series a volume on "Bacteria and their Products".

When the Research Laboratories of the Royal College of Physicians of Edinburgh were established in 1887, he was the first superintendent and organized them; but three years later he left Edinburgh to become the first director of the laboratories of the Royal College of Physicians of London and of the Royal College of Surgeons of England. During the next nine years he placed the manufacture of diphtheria antitoxin in this country on a sound basis, and carried out investigations for the Royal Commission on Tuberculosis appointed in 1890. In 1897 the British Medical Association awarded him the Stewart Prize for work in connection with the origin and spread of epidemic

PROFESSOR SIR GERMAN SIMS WOODHEAD
K.B.E., M.D.

disease. He started the *Journal of Pathology and Bacteriology* in 1893 and was sole editor until 1906, when with the establishment of the Pathological Society of Great Britain and Ireland they became associated; he continued to be editor-in-chief, though no longer the sole editor, until he resigned in 1920 and the Journal was transferred to the Society.

After Kanthack's death Woodhead was elected Professor of Pathology and a fellow of Trinity Hall in 1899; he was appointed a member of the Royal Commission on Tuberculosis set up in September 1901. He was instrumental in starting the Field Laboratories at Cambridge, investigated the continuous temperature of tuberculous patients by Gamgee's method at Addenbrooke's Hospital (with P. C. Varrier-Jones), and installed an electro-cardiograph in his laboratory, which was later connected by a special cable with Addenbrooke's hospital. Like Kanthack, he was mainly a morbid anatomist and bacteriologist, and thus differed from Roy who was essentially an experimental physiologist and pathologist. As already mentioned, he organized the new pathological department in the Medical School, opened in 1904. He played an important part in directions other than pathology, such as the cause of temperance, being President of the British Medical Temperance Association and of the British Temperance League, and with Varrier-Jones the organization of the Tuberculosis Colony, first at Bourn (1916) and then at Papworth (1918), near Cambridge. During the War he was extremely active, first as a sanitary officer, then as adviser to the War Office, and in 1917 as Inspector of Laboratories in

Military Hospitals throughout the United Kingdom. For his services he was created K.B.E. in June 1919. Birmingham and Toronto conferred on him the honorary LL.D. degree. He was President of the Royal Microscopical Society (1913–1916), and took a keen interest in the Pathological and Bacteriological Laboratory Assistants' Association, which was founded in 1912, was its president (1916–1921), and has his name kept in remembrance by the Association's Sims Woodhead Prize.

He died suddenly at Aisthorpe Hall, Lincolnshire, on December 29, 1921.

REFERENCES

Brit. Med. Journ. 1922, i, 39, 81.
Journ. Path. and Bacteriol. Edin. 1922, xxv, 118–37.
Memoir (a Collection of Obituary Notices and Tributes), published privately, Edinburgh, 1923.

VII. *Department of the Quick Chair of Biology*

THIS professorship was established by a Grace of May 10, 1906, which provided that the professor should devote himself to the study of the protozoa, especially such as cause disease; but in 1920, on the recommendation of the Managers of the Quick Fund, this definition of the professor's duty was broadened to the study of parasitology. By the will of Frederick James Quick (1836–1902), of Trinity Hall (B.A. 1859), a wholesale tea merchant much interested in biology and botany, funds were left for the stipend (£1000) of a professor and eventually for a sum not to exceed £300 for expenses and assistance. The professorial stipend was, like others, subsequently raised to £1200. The chair, which is tenable for three years, the holder being subject to re-election, was filled in 1906 by George Henry Falkiner Nuttall, who earlier in that year had been appointed to the Readership in Hygiene established by Grace of May 24, 1906, having previously been University Lecturer in Bacteriology and Preventive Medicine since September 29, 1900. He was successively re-elected to the chair until the end of the academic year 1930–1.

By Grace of December 17, 1908, the Office of Assistant to the Quick Professor was established by the University, and by Grace of May 16, 1919, a second assistantship was authorized, but subsequently lapsed. A University Lectureship was established by Grace of May 29, 1925, and filled by the appointment of D. Keilin of Magdalene College.

From 1907 to 1921 the Quick Laboratory consisted of one large room, divided into cubicles, on the ground floor of the Medical School in Downing Street; in 1909–10 a field laboratory was established with the help of private benefactions on the Milton Road. The laboratory accommodation in the Medical School soon became inadequate, and in May 1919 the Quick Professor issued an appeal on *The Need for an Institute for Parasitological Research in Cambridge*. This evoked an immediate and most generous response from Mr and Mrs P. A. Molteno, who had previously given financial assistance in 1909 and 1914, and did so subsequently in 1924. The Molteno Institute for Research in Parasitology was formally opened on November 28, 1921, by Earl Buxton of Newtimber. Its cost (£35,406) including equipment was met by Mr and Mrs P. A. Molteno.

Nuttall founded the *Journal of Hygiene*, the first number of which appeared in January 1901, and *Parasitology*, which began as a supplement of the *Journal of Hygiene* in 1908.

The Managers of the Frederick James Quick Fund reported on April 9, 1931, that the next tenure of the Quick Chair should be associated with the study of the biology of the cell, and that the chair should be offered to D. Keilin; this was approved by Grace of May 22, 1931.

REFERENCES

Historical Register of the University of Cambridge, edited by J. R. TANNER, pp. 108–9, Cambridge, 1917.

NUTTALL, G. H. F. "The Molteno Institute for Research in Parasitology, University of Cambridge", *Methods and Problems of Medical Education* (Third Series), 1925, pp. 189–94, Rockefeller Foundation, New York. Also information from him.

Cambridge University Reporter 1931, LXI, 965, 1079.

VIII. *The Regius Chair of Physic*

FIVE Regius Professorships—of Divinity, Civil Law, Physic, Hebrew, Greek—were founded in 1540, nearly at the same time as the destruction of the monasteries, by Henry VIII, who was described by Hastings Rashdall as "that munificent donor of other people's property". The stipend of each was £40 per annum, in those days a very adequate provision and more than four times as much as that assigned in 1546 by the same founder to a fellow of Trinity, including all his allowances. The Royal Letters Patent under the Great Seal on the appointment of the Regius Professor of Physic in 1925 gave the salary of thirty-four pounds and eighteen shillings "of good and lawful money of Great Britain" (£40 less fees) to "the Instructor in the Science of Physic". A sixth Regius Professorship—of Modern History—was instituted in 1724 by George I.

Up to 1900 the five original Regius chairs had the following number of incumbents:[1]

Divinity	30	with an average duration of tenure of				12 years	
Civil Law	25	,,	,,	,,	,,	14·5	,,
Physic	18	,,	,,	,,	,,	20	,,
Hebrew	25	,,	,,	,,	,,	14·5	,,
Greek	30	,,	,,	,,	,,	12	,,

1 At Oxford, where five Regius Professorships with similar stipends were founded in 1546, the incumbents of the chairs up to 1900 number as follows: Divinity 34, Hebrew 24, Greek 27, Medicine 20, Civil Law, 21. The differences in the average tenure of office are less striking than at Cambridge: Medicine $17\frac{3}{4}$, Civil Law $16\frac{5}{6}$, Hebrew $14\frac{1}{2}$, Greek 13, and Divinity $10\frac{1}{3}$ years.

The longer tenure of office by the Professors of Physic might, and perhaps with some reason, be ascribed to their obedience to the direction "physician, heal thyself", but this is not the whole explanation. The shorter periods of tenure by the Professors of Divinity, Civil Law, Hebrew, and Greek would appear to have been due in the main to translation to some higher or more lucrative office, whereas almost all the Professors of Physic were local physicians, and with few exceptions (Blyth, Hatcher, and Bond) occupied their chairs until their dying day.

The average age on appointment works out at forty-seven, the extremes being sixty-three (Paget) and thirty-two years (Plumptre, who held the chair for the record period of fifty-two years, and Haviland, who was in occupation for thirty-four years). Some of the holders of the chair enjoyed the position for lengthy periods; two Regius Professors—Green (1700–1741) and Plumptre (1741–1793)—practically divided the eighteenth century between them, and in the previous century Glisson, the most distinguished in the list, was appointed at the age of thirty-nine and held office for forty-one years. On the other hand Hatcher and Winterton were professors for one year only. Five of the Regius Professors—Glisson (*aet.* 80), Green (90), Plumptre (84), Paget (83), and Allbutt (89)—were in office when eighty or more years of age, a survival of the fittest which never can happen again, for all Cambridge professors appointed after October 1, 1924, will vacate their office and become Emeritus Professors at the end of the academic year in which they attain the age of sixty-five years. In other words, whereas in the past a professor's efficiency might expire before his official death, in the future it will be possible for his official removal to precede the advent of senile incapacity. The average age at death or resignation (Blyth, Hatcher, and Bond) of the first eighteen Regius Professors of Physic works out as $67\frac{1}{4}$ years.

Of the eighteen professors appointed between 1540 and 1900, Gonville and Caius College claims seven, two of whom were also its Masters and for a time Members of Parliament (Gostlin for Barnstaple, and Brady for the University); King's provided four professors, all in the first hundred years of the professorship, but Robert Glynn Clobery (1719–1800) of that house, the medical attendant of Thomas Gray the poet, is known to have declined the chair in 1793, when offered it by William Pitt whom he had attended in 1773. He was an extremely kind though eccentric soul, whose features belied his character, so of him it was written:

> This morning, quite dead, Tom was found in his bed
> Although he was hearty last night,
> But 'tis thought, having seen Dr Glynn in his dreams,
> That the poor fellow died of the fright.

St John's contributed one occupant of the chair during each of the first four centuries, and Peterhouse, Queens', and Corpus each one since 1540. None of the first nineteen Regius Professors of Physic came from Trinity, which supplied eleven of the thirty Regius Professors of Divinity, sixteen out of the twenty-five of Hebrew, and twenty-three out of the thirty of Greek. The professorships of Divinity, Hebrew, and Greek form part of the foundation of Trinity College, the Statutes given to that

ROBERT GLYNN CLOBERY, M.D.

college by Queen Mary directing that it should pay the stipends of these professors.

The stipend of the Regius Professor of Physic was increased from the original £40, partly by a house and premises in the parish of Great St Mary's, bequeathed to the University by John Crane (1572–1652), apothecary and Sheriff of Cambridgeshire, for the use of the Professor. In this benefaction Crane followed the example of James I, who in 1617 had augmented the income of the Regius Professor of Medicine at Oxford by annexing to the chair the Mastership of the alms-houses at Ewelme in Oxfordshire. In 1724 the site of the house left by Crane was required for the building of the Senate House, and it was exchanged for property in Market Street. In 1872 the Regius Professor's stipend was made up in various ways— the ancient Government stipend £34 18s. 0d. (£40 less fees), the rent of Crane's house £130, compensation for fees of M.B. £50, and £35 from the University Chest in lieu of share of professorial fund, and, in addition to this fixed sum of £249 18s. 0d., ten guineas for each Act for M.D. and three guineas for each candidate entering for the first M.B. examination. In February 1873 the Council of the Senate recommended that in addition to the ancient stipend and the rent of Crane's house the Regius Professor should receive £300 annually, and two guineas a term from each student attending his lectures. Under the Statutes of the University approved by the Queen in Council on June 29, 1882, the Regius Professor received £700 a year, made up by the ancient stipend, the rent of Crane's house, and the balance from the University Chest; this stipend was subject to a deduction of £200 if the Professor was the Master or a fellow of a college. Under the Grace of October 31, 1919, the property (Crane's house) held for the trust was sold and the proceeds invested by the Ministry of Agriculture and Fisheries. For three years the stipend was then in excess of £1200 per annum, but since 1923 it has been £1200, at which sum it was definitely fixed in June 1926.

Crane also endowed a fund (Crane's Charity) to relieve poor sick scholars, which remained in abeyance until 1822 but is now of the greatest assistance to men living on the limited income derived from scholarships when they are taken ill and have to meet unexpected expenses caused thereby.

The first eighteen Regius Professors of Physic present a considerable diversity of gifts. Some, such as Winterton (1600–1636) and Ward (1584–1609), were pre-eminently scholars, thus corresponding with the spirit of Linacre and the contemporary scholar-physicians. At a later date Glisson (1597–1677) in addition to being a scholar was in the forefront, even in advance, of the science of the times, and was President of the Royal College of Physicians of London. In the present century Allbutt combined the attributes of a classical scholar with the full sympathy of a modern scientific physician. Out of the eighteen Regius Professors, fourteen are noticed in the *Dictionary of National Biography*, ten out of the last eleven being there represented; three—Glisson, Paget, and Allbutt—were fellows of the Royal Society; four—Pennington, Haviland, Paget, and Allbutt—delivered the Harveian Oration at the Royal College of Physicians of London. Until 1892 the chair was always filled from the comparatively narrow circle of medical graduates resident in Cambridge, and some of the occupants were more prominent in University affairs than in medical science; thus Hatcher and Gostlin were Vice-Chancellors, and, as already mentioned, Gostlin and Brady were Masters of Gonville and Caius College.

On November 8, 1590, just half a century after the foundation of the five original Regius Professors by Henry VIII, Robert Cooke, Clarencieux King of Arms, granted by letters patent at the request of Thomas Lorkin, Regius Professor of Physic (1564–1591), to the Regius Professors "and their successors in lyke place and office for euer" official arms and crests. Those for the Regius Professor of Physic are: "*Arms*: azure a fess ermine and three lozenges gold; on a chief gules a gold leopard charged on the side with the letter M sable. *Crest*: on a wreath gold and azure a silver quinquangle" (Tanner). The description given by St John Hope is worded in slightly different terms: "*Arms*: azure, a fess ermine, between three lozenges or a chief gules, a lion passant gardant gold charged on the side with the letter M sable. *Crest*: on a wreath or and azure, a quinquangle argent". The University had previously, on June 9, 1573, received from Robert Cooke a grant of arms: "gules a cross ermine and four gold leopards with a book gules upon the cross". The motto of the University "Hinc lucem et pocula sacra" was used at the end of the sixteenth century by John Legate, the elder, University printer (1588–1609) (Stokes).

REFERENCES

Historical Register of the University of Cambridge, edited by J. R. TANNER, pp. 71, 85, Cambridge, 1917.

HOPE, W. H. ST. J. *Proc. Camb. Antiquar. Soc.* 1891–4, VIII, 130.

STOKES, H. P. *The Emblem, the Arms and Motto of the University of Cambridge*, Cambridge, 1928.

REGIUS PROFESSORS OF PHYSIC

	Appointed
John Blyth	1540
John Hatcher	1554
Henry Walker	1555
Thomas Lorkin	1564
William Ward	1591
William Burton	1596
John Gostlin	1623
John Collins	1626
Ralph Winterton	1635
Francis Glisson	1636
Robert Brady	1677
Christopher Green	1700
Russell Plumptre	1741
Sir Isaac Pennington	1794
John Haviland	1817
Henry John Hayles Bond	1851
Sir George Paget	1872
Sir Thomas Clifford Allbutt	1892
Sir Humphry Davy Rolleston	1925

Regius Professor 1540–1554

John Blyth or Blythe, the first Regius Professor of Physic, who came of a Derbyshire stock, was born at Sheffield. Educated at Eton, he was admitted a scholar at King's on August 12, 1520, in due course became a fellow (1523), and proceeded to the degrees of B.A. (1524–5) and M.A. (1528). Like Caius, he was first in the *Ordo Senioritatis*, out of which the Mathematical Tripos gradually evolved, the actual change in name taking place in 1747–8. As one of the proctors he was largely responsible for the conduct of the *Ordo Senioritatis* in 1529–30. He then travelled widely on the Continent, visited Germany, Louvain, Padua, and Ferrara, and took the doctorate of medicine at the last-named University on May 23, 1533. This degree is said to have been considered in his favour as regards the appointment to the Regius chair; but an influential factor was probably his marriage to Alice, sister of Sir John Cheke (1514–1557), the last "Master of the Glomery" (1539–40), a University officer who controlled and on occasion collected (*glomerare = congregare* [T. Baker]) the students (glomerels) who with the intention of becoming schoolmasters took the old-time degree in grammar, *glomerie*, according to W. W. Skeat, being a perversion of *grammaire* (Stokes); this separate degree died out after 1548. Cheke was also the first Regius Professor of Greek (1540–1547), Public

Orator (1542–1546), Provost of King's (1548–1553), and a power in the University. He was, it may be noted, eighteenth in the *Ordo Senioritatis* (1529–30) when Blyth was proctor. It has been suggested that William Turner, botanist, physician, and Dean of Wells (1550), who left Cambridge finally in 1540, was disappointed in not being elected to the chair. Blyth became M.D. Cambridge (by incorporation from Ferrara) in 1543. The letters patent announcing his appointment in 1540 use the phrase "Reader in Medicine", not Professor. Harwood's *Alumni Etonenses* states that "for his excellent skill and judgment in that faculty (physic) he was elected by the consent of the whole University Regius Professor of Physic". On May 11, 1554, he was confirmed in the Regius chair by letters patent, Queen Mary; but later in the same year he resigned. In the following year he subscribed to the Roman Catholic articles then imposed on all graduates. In 1552 he took part, according to Fuller, in an episode showing the disturbed state of the times; Edwin Sandys (1516?–1588), when in his seat as Vice-Chancellor in the Regent House, was attacked by "one Master Mitch with a rabble of some twenty papists"; being a man of spirit he "groped for his dagger" and would have dispatched several of them had he not been restrained by the prayers and entreaties of Blyth and William Bill, then Master of Trinity (1551–1553), who had previously been Linacre Lecturer (1547–1549) and concurrently Master of St John's (1546–1551). The date of Blyth's death is not known, but he was alive in 1557.

REFERENCES

BAKER, T. *History of the College of St John the Evangelist, Cambridge*, edited by J. E. B. MAYOR, part I, p. 28–30, Cambridge, 1869.

FULLER, T. *The History of the University of Cambridge from the Conquest to the Year 1634*, p. 251, edition 1840.

STOKES, H. P. *Ceremonies of the University of Cambridge*, p. 75, Cambridge, 1927.

JOHN HATCHER (1512–1587), M.D.

Regius Professor 1554–1555

The second Regius Professor was remarkable in several respects; he retired from the chair, to which he was appointed probably in 1554, after a year's tenure; he amassed a considerable fortune and lived in "almost a princely style of magnificence" (Palmer), and was Vice-Chancellor of the University in 1579–1580, although he was not Master of a college. It may be noted that in 1586, after the election as Vice-Chancellor of John Copcot, fellow of Trinity "within which he gave the upper hand to Dr John Still (then Master) but took it out of him when out of the college", it was enacted that "for the time to come none but heads of houses should be chosen vice-chancellors". Hatcher came from Surrey, probably from Croydon, and entering St John's College took the degree of B.A., being twenty-second in the *Ordo Senioritatis* 1531–2, was elected a fellow of that college on March 31, 1533, and proceeded to the degrees of M.A. in 1535 and M.D. in 1543–4. In 1557 he was member of a Syndicate to reform the election of the proctors and to revise the ancient Statutes of the University. He first married Alice, daughter of Edward Green of London, and had one son, Thomas (*obiit* 1583), an antiquary to whom Caius in 1570 inscribed his *De Libris propriis*, and who is noticed in the *Dictionary of National Biography*, although the Regius Professor is omitted; of his two daughters one, Catherine, became the wife of another Regius Professor of Physic, Thomas Lorkin. In 1582 he married again, this time a widow, Jane Freville, but this was not a success, for his will, executed less than two years later, stated that she had "most undutifully stept aside from him, without his consent or knowledge", and his legacy to her of a black gown was conditional on her wearing it at his funeral.

The Computus rolls of Peterhouse show that in 1544 Hatcher was the tenant, at a rent of eight shillings a year, of "the soler over the almose howse" in Great St Mary's parish, and make it probable that he added the trades of apothecary and of a dry goods merchant to the profession of curing the sick; he is there described as "the punctual and thrifty doctor". On December 10, 1545, he bought from George Keinsham the extensive grounds and buildings of the recently suppressed Augustinian or Austin friary, which extended from what is now Bene't Street to Downing Street; he lived there until his death in March 1586–7, and was buried in St Edward's Church on March 24. The house was immense with twenty-seven rooms, the "great parlour", probably the original refectory, being seventy yards long; it became ruinous and in 1783 was sold by the University to John Mortlock (1755–

1816) of Great Abingdon. The Mansion House, part of the old Monastery, and five acres of the grounds were bought for £1600 in 1760 and presented to the University by an enthusiastic botanist, the Rev. Richard Walker (1679–1764), D.D., Vice-Master of Trinity, and were occupied by the Public Physic Garden until it was removed, between 1846 and 1852, to its present site. Hatcher left funds to local charities, bequeathed a rent charge of forty shillings a year for the care of the clock which he erected in Great St Mary's and, in default of male issue, the friary property to the University to found a hall for students to be called Hatcher's Hall, but this was never carried into effect. Soon after Hatcher's death the Austin friary passed into the hands of Stephen Perse (1548–1615), M.D., Senior Fellow of Caius, who left over £14,000 personal estate with landed property in addition, and part of the site for a free Grammar School (the first Perse School), in what is now Free School Lane; in 1890 the school was removed to Hills Road. Hatcher was one of the Visitors, at any rate in 1571, of Gonville and Caius College.

Hatcher also acquired the Manor of Careby, near Stamford in Lincolnshire, and an estate at Little Bytham in the same county. His only literary contribution seems to have been some Latin verses in the memoir and collection of tributes to Henry and Charles Brandon, the two young Dukes of Suffolk of St John's College, who both died from the sweating sickness in the Bishop of Lincoln's Palace at Buckden in Huntingdonshire on July 16, 1551, the younger surviving the elder by about half an hour, so that he also was a duke. Hatcher left a large classical library containing many theological, medical, and legal works.

REFERENCES

COOPER, C. H. *Athenae Cantabrigienses*, II, 7, Cambridge, 1861.
PALMER, W. M. *Camb. Antiquar. Soc. Communications*, 1911, XV, 238–45.
Peterhouse Biographical Register, by T. A. WALKER, part I, 1284–1574, pp. 142–3, Cambridge, 1927.

HENRY WALKER (1503?–1564), M.D.

Regius Professor 1555–1564

About the life of Henry Walker, the third Regius Professor, details, for example about his exact age, are rather scanty. He was a member of Gonville Hall, and is mentioned by John Caius (1510–1573) as a contemporary. He took the degree of B.A., being fifteenth in the *Ordo Senioritatis* of 1524–5, the year in which his predecessor Blyth headed the list; so if, like Blyth, he was then about twenty-one years of age, he would have been born in 1503, or seven years before Caius. He proceeded to the degree of M.A. (1528), and in 1531–2 was incorporated M.D. from the University of Angers. He was appointed Regius Professor about 1555, and held this post until his death in April 1564. Together with Hatcher he was, on September 26, 1556, on a Commission of the Peace for the University and the Town of Cambridge. A zealous Catholic, he signed the Marian articles in 1555 and took an active part in the proceedings connected with Cardinal

Pole's (1500–1558) visitation of the University in 1556, when he was one of the Commissioners appointed to inquire about heresies and heretical books. He had landed property at Langham, Norfolk, and left his books—sixty-eight in number—to Gonville and Caius College. His son, George Walker (1533–1597) was one of the "repliers" in the Physic Act kept in Great St Mary's on August 7 before Queen Elizabeth, when she visited Cambridge in 1564, the year in which he took the degree of M.D. John Caius, ex-President, and Robert Huicke, President of the Royal College of Physicians of London, also took part, besides the then Regius Professor, Thomas Lorkin, and, according to Cooper, Frere (? Thomas Fryer) in these medical disputations.

REFERENCES

COOPER, C. H. *Athenae Cantabrigienses*, I, 231, Cambridge, 1858.
    Annals of Cambridge, II, 108, 196, Cambridge, 1843.
VENN, J. *Biographical History of Gonville and Caius College*
    (1349–1897), I, 27, Cambridge, 1897.

THOMAS LORKIN (1528?–1591), M.D.

Regius Professor 1564–1591

Thomas Lorkin or Lorkyn, the son of Thomas Lorkin and his wife Joan Huxley, was born at Frindsbury, Kent, probably in 1528. At Michaelmas 1549 he matriculated as a pensioner at Pembroke Hall, but migrated to Queens' College where he was a scholar and, being seventeenth in the *Ordo Senioritatis* 1551–2, took the degree of B.A. and became a fellow (1551–1553). He then moved again, following Andrew Perne (1519?–1589), previously a fellow of Queens', to Peterhouse where he became a probationer fellow on November 11, 1553, and on November 14 of the following year a fellow (1554–1561); he proceeded to the degree of M.A. (1555), and took the licence to practise physic (M.L.) in 1559. In the following year he proceeded to the degree of M.D., and married at St Edward's Church on November 15, 1560, Catherine, daughter of John Hatcher. Catherine, one of his five daughters, became about 1578 the wife of Edward Lively (1545?–1605), who was Regius Professor of Hebrew (1575–1605) and one of the forty-seven learned men appointed in 1604 by James I to make an "authorized" translation of the Bible, being President of the second division of the translators, which sat at Cambridge. Towards the end of his life Lorkin appears to have had rooms in Trinity Hall.

On April 21, 1564, Lorkin was constituted Regius Professor of Physic for life by Queen's letters patent; and on August 7 during Queen Elizabeth's visit to Cambridge took the "responsall's" seat at the medical disputations in Great St Mary's when John Caius, as "antient in that faculty" moved the following questions: (1) "An cibus simplex sit praeferendus multiplici", and (2) "An coena prandio liberalior esse debeat".

In 1570 the Elizabethan Statutes superseded the *Statuta antiqua* under which medical students were required either to take a degree in Arts or to spend some years in studying the subjects for an Arts degree before becoming bachelors of medicine; for the degree of M.D.

an Arts degree was compulsory. The Elizabethan Statutes removed the requirements of a preliminary training in Arts and allowed students to start medical work directly they came up. The result of this was that after a time the medical graduates commonly did not take a degree in Arts (*vide* p. 24), and their liberal education was curtailed. Lorkin and his successor, the scholarly Ward, were among the one hundred and sixty-four members of the University who on May 6, 1572, presented a petition to the Chancellor against the Statutes which mainly aroused opposition on grounds other than the medical changes. The petition was dismissed by a committee consisting of the two archbishops and three bishops, and with but little modification these regulations remained in force until 1859.

Lorkin subscribed when young to the Roman Catholic articles and in later years opposed puritan preaching in the University. It was due to his action that in 1590 a grant by letters patent of arms and crests was made to the five Regius Professors (*vide* p. 125). His own arms were: Ermine three lions' heads erased A. He was the author of a tract of seventeen pages, *Recta Regula et Victus ratio pro Studiosis et Literatis*, 8vo, London, 1562, dedicated to the Master (Andrew Perne, Dean of Ely) and fellows of Peterhouse. His "Carmen Latinum decastichon" is affixed to the Cottonian manuscript "Historia Anglicana" of John Herd, M.D. (1512?–1588). His generosity to the poor and other charities earned for him the description "the philanthropic Professor of Physic".

He died on May 1, 1591, and was buried in Great St Mary's Church, Cambridge, where there is a memorial brass to him. He left certain lands to his daughters and their heirs for ever, but if they died without issue (which they did not, for Catherine Lively had eleven children) Pembroke Hall, Queens' College, and Peterhouse were to benefit. His medical books, about 272 in number, were left to the University Library, to be kept "in a great cupboard locked"; of these eight were incunabula and only four were in English. He also directed that a sermon should be preached for him yearly and that 6s. 8d. should be paid to the preacher.

REFERENCES

PALMER, W. M. *Camb. Antiquar. Soc. Communications*, 1911, XV, 245–7.
Peterhouse Biographical Register, by T. A. WALKER, part I, 1284–1574, pp. 192, 268, Cambridge, 1927.

WILLIAM WARD (1534–1609), M.D.

Regius Professor 1591–1609

William Ward or Warde was born at Landbeach, Cambridgeshire, in 1534, and after education at Eton was elected a scholar at King's College, Cambridge, on August 13, 1550. On February 27, 1551, the Provost of King's requested him to take up the study of medicine. He proceeded to the degree of B.A., being thirtieth in the *Ordo Senioritatis* for 1554–5, and to the degrees of M.A. in 1558 and M.D. in 1567. He was a fellow of King's from 1553 to 1568, being admitted before he took his degree, for in those days scholars of King's were promoted

137

as a matter of course on completion of their "three probationary years". He was bursar of the college 1559–1563. In 1591 he became Regius Professor of Physic, but subsequent letters patent, dated November 8, 1596, show that this office was then to be shared with a junior fellow of King's—William Burton. The statement to the effect that Ward was physician to Queen Elizabeth and James I was probably a mistaken interpretation of the title Regius Professor of Physic. More eminent as a scholar than as a medical man, Ward translated "The Secretes of the Reverende Maister Alexis Piemont containing excellent remedies against divers diseases", parts I, II, and III, 1558, 1560, 1562, from the French, and from the Latin "The most excellent, profitable and pleasaunt Booke of the famous doctor and expert astrologer Arcandam or Aleandrin", 1578. In 1590 he gave $7\frac{1}{2}$ acres of arable land in Howsfoeld and two acres of meadow in Chesterton to the parish of Great St Mary's; he was buried in that church on August 8, 1609. The manuscript catalogue of the Provosts, Fellows, and Scholars of King's College, Cambridge, drawn up about 1750 by Antony Allen, contains the following encomium: "Ward was accounted an excellent, judicious, and careful phisitian, a good housekeeper, and an honest and true-hearted man".

REFERENCES

COOPER, C. H. *Athenae Cantabrigienses*, II, 386, Cambridge, 1861.
Information from the Records of King's College, Cambridge, provided by John Saltmarsh.

WILLIAM BURTON (1560–1623), M.D.

Regius Professor 1596–1623

William Burton, the son of Richard Burton of Cashelt (Carshalton), Surrey, was educated at Eton and was elected a scholar of King's College on August 25, 1578, being then eighteen years old. So far his record was much the same as that of his predecessor, Ward; but the college records show that on May 27, 1582, he was warned to correct his former negligence in the study of the Greek tongue, and that on August 12, 1586, he was sharply rebuked for irreverent and quarrelsome conduct in Hall on pain of withdrawal of victuals. He had, however, already become a fellow in the ordinary course on August 26, 1581, and taken the degrees of B.A. (1582–3) and of M.A. (1586). The records further state that on October 31, 1590, he was "diverted to the Astronomy", and was a College Lecturer 1583–1585, and Dean of Arts and Lecturer on Philosophy 1590–1 and 1592–3; but he proceeded to the M.D. degree at an unknown date. He vacated his fellowship in 1594. Ward and Burton were jointly appointed "Readers in Medicine or the Medical Art" (Regius Professors of Physic) by letters patent dated November 8, 1596, with a stipend of £40, and as Ward died in 1609 Burton held office alone from that date. It may well be that the scholarly Ward was glad to delegate his professorial duties to a junior, and found a convenient deputy in a medical fellow of his own college. Burton, who does not appear to have contributed to medical literature, died suddenly in the Regent House on June 11, 1623.

139

REFERENCES

Information from the Records of King's College, Cambridge, provided by John Saltmarsh.

TANNER, J. R. *Historical Register of the University of Cambridge to the Year 1910*, p. 80, Cambridge, 1917.

JOHN GOSTLIN (1566?–1626), M.D.

Regius Professor 1623–1626

John Gostlin or Gostlyn was born in Norwich about 1566, as the son of Robert Gostlin, Sheriff of that city in 1570, and was educated at the Cathedral Grammar School. On November 22, 1582, when sixteen years of age, he entered Gonville and Caius College, where he was a scholar for eight years. He proceeded to the degrees of B.A., being twentieth in the *Ordo Senioritatis* 1586–7, M.A. (1590), and M.D. (1602), being incorporated M.D. at Oxford July 14, 1612. On Lady Day 1592 he was admitted a fellow and filled most of the college offices, was a proctor in 1600, and retained his fellowship until he eventually became Master in February 1618–9. After the death of Dr Thomas Legge on July 12, 1607, Gostlin was the popular and natural successor, and the fellows without any delay chose him for the vacant Mastership; but the Chancellor of the University, Robert Cecil, Earl of Salisbury, summarily set aside their recommendation on the ground of an irregularity in the procedure, and on December 14 inducted William Branthwaite, D.D., a fellow of Emmanuel, who was a good Hebrew scholar and

140

translated the Apocrypha for the revised version of the Bible (1607–1611). Feeling this rebuff acutely, Gostlin left Cambridge to practise medicine at Exeter, and in 1614 was returned as Member of Parliament for Barnstaple. In March of the following year James I and his son Henry, Prince of Wales, visited Cambridge, and Gostlin was summoned by the general request of the heads of colleges as the fittest person to take the part of "respondent" in the medical disputation to be held before the King. In deference, no doubt, to the King's "Counterblast to Tobacco" (1604) the tenth order for the preparations against the Royal visit provided: "that no Graduate, Scholler, or Student of this Universitie presume to resort to any Inn, Taverne, Ale-howse, or Tobacco-shop, at any tyme dureing the abode of his Majestie here; nor doe presume to take tobacco in St Marie's Church (at the Act) or in Trinity Colledge Hall (at the performance of *Aemilia, Ignoramus, Albumazar,* and *Melanthe*), upon payne of finall expellinge the Universitie". In January 1618–9 William Branthwaite, then Vice-Chancellor, died of consumption at Badlingham, Newmarket, and again the fellows of Gonville and Caius at once selected Gostlin for the vacant Mastership. But being suspected of Roman Catholic sympathies he was not in favour at Court, and the fellows' nomination was followed by a letter from James I recommending Sir Thomas Wilson (1560?–1629), Keeper of the State Records. The college authorities, however, persisted, and with the powerful influence of George Mountain (1569–1628), Bishop of Lincoln, carried the day so that Gostlin, then at Exeter, became the twentieth Master of the college on February

16, 1618–9, his joy at returning to Cambridge being described as "almost excessive" (Venn).

On June 25, 1623, he was appointed Regius Professor, the official entry (Calendar of State Papers, Domestic, 1623, p. 619) recording a grant to "Dr John Gostlin for life of the office of Reader of physic lectures at Cambridge". This has been ascribed to the backing he received from a letter written on June 12, the day after Burton's death, by Isaac Barrow, M.D., fellow of Trinity (not the famous divine and fellow of Trinity), to John Packer (1570?–1649), clerk of the privy seal, asking for his assistance in obtaining the physic Reader's place for Gostlin who was "without question the moste worthie man of his profession in the Universitie, and one that is moste desired of all". This was followed by a certificate from the Vice-Chancellor and nearly all the heads of colleges. Gostlin does not appear to have published anything, but the library of Gonville and Caius contains MSS. notes of his medical lectures and disputations. He was not a fellow of the Royal College of Physicians of London. Like Hatcher he was Vice-Chancellor, but on two occasions, though in neither did he serve for the whole term; first in 1619 to take the place of William Branthwaite who died in office, and again in 1625 until his own death in the early part of the academic year 1626–7. During his Vice-Chancellorships there were two decrees showing the difference between those times and the present day; in 1619 "he made it a heavy fine for any undergraduate to wear boots"; one bold spirit, however, bet that he would do so while visiting the Vice-Chancellor, and carried it off by asking for advice about numbness in the legs asserted to be hereditary; "the Vice-Chancellor pitying instead of punishing him, prescribed him his best receipts" (T. Fuller). In 1625 the heads of the colleges prohibited the admission of bedmakers, illiterate men and boys, and even women into the colleges to perform the menial services which previously had been a source of income to poor scholars. Like Branthwaite, he died in office, breathing his last in college on October 21, 1626. His funeral was delayed until November 16 when he was buried in the college chapel where there is a monument to his memory. Milton, then an undergraduate at Christ's College, wrote a Latin ode "In Obitum Procancellarii" on the occasion. Gostlin's portrait, showing features described by William Moore (1574–1659), the "completer" of the college *Annals*, as "somewhat resembling those of a lion", hangs in the Master's Lodge. He was a benefactor to his own college, where a court was called after him, and to St Catharine's Hall he left the Bull Inn, having bequeathed another inn, the Rose and Crown, to his own college. Fuller wrote "After Thomas Bacon, fifteenth Master of the Colledge (Gonville and Caius), had been a Malefactour thereunto, leaving it much indebted, the four succeeding Masters (ill examples avoided do good) Dr Caius, Legge, Branthwaite, Gostlin (all natives of Norwich) were signall Benefactours, though Masters of, but Stewards for the House; making it, for the main, their Heir, at their decease". Of all the Regius Professors of Physic Gostlin held the most varied non-professional positions of eminence, for he was a Member of Parliament, Master of a College, and twice Vice-Chancellor of the University.

FULLER, T. *The History of the Worthies of England*, pp. 275, 277, London, 1662.

VENN, J. *Biographical History of Gonville and Caius College* (1349–1901), III, 74–85, Cambridge, 1901.

JOHN COLLINS (1572–1634), M.D., F.R.C.P.

Regius Professor 1626–1634

John Collins coming from Surrey matriculated as a sizar at St John's College in 1591, was admitted a scholar on November 9, 1592, and a fellow on April 7, 1598. He proceeded to the degrees of B.A. (1595–6), M.A. (1599), and M.D. (1608), and was Linacre lecturer for four years (1600–1604). Helkiah Crooke (1576–1635), his contemporary as a scholar, was physician to James I, to whom he dedicated a compilation with the imposing title *Mikrokosmographia*: *A Description of the Body of Man*, 1616 (second edition, 1631). Crooke, like Collins, did not take any notice of Harvey's discovery of the circulation, thus confirming Harvey's rather pathetic remark that no one over forty years of age accepted his views. Collins was the first Regius Professor to become a fellow of the Royal College of Physicians of London, being admitted a "candidate" on the day after Palm Sunday, 1611, and a fellow on May 7, 1613; in 1615 he was a censor and in 1624 anatomy lecturer, a post superseded by or merged in the Goulstonian lectureship soon after 1666.

On November 8, 1626, he was appointed Regius

Professor, and almost at once, presumably not from slackness on his part, attention was called to negligence of the Regius Professors with regard to making one "anatomy" during the year. On January 28, 1627, a Grace was passed making provisions for more efficient teaching in the subject. From February 1629 to November 1630 Cambridge suffered one of its most considerable visitations from the plague and, though the death-rate (347 out of 617 from all causes) was comparatively low, including perhaps Thomas Goade, one of the proctors, the colleges were dispersed. Apparently there was some complacency about the granting of degrees in this emergency; for, according to Fuller,

this corruption of the air proved the generation of many doctors, graduated in a clandestine way, without keeping any acts, to the great disgust of those who had fairly gotten their degrees with public pains and expence. Yea, Dr Collins, being afterwards to admit an able man doctor, did (according to the pleasantness of his fancy) distinguish "inter cathedram pestilentiae, et cathedram eminentiae", leaving it to his auditors easily to apprehend his meaning therein.

As will be seen, his successor Winterton had very strong views about such relaxations (*vide* p. 150). Collins died at Cambridge in December 1634, and was buried in the old chapel of St John's College on December 14. By his will, dated December 8 of that year and proved on December 24, he left most of his "physick Books", including a fine manuscript of Oribasius, and £100 to buy more, to the College. This donation-book-plate in Collins's books is one of the earliest book-plates, at least in Great Britain, for in Germany twelve medical book-plates of the sixteenth century are known.[1] To his apprentice he left a grey coat, an old shirt, and several books, such as Gerard's *Herbal*, Vigo's *Surgery*, and the *Pharmacopoeia Londinensis*, and all his brewing vessels. To Dr R. Winterton he bequeathed books and clothes, including a black cloth coat lined with plush.

REFERENCES

FULLER, T. *History of the University of Cambridge from the Conquest to the year 1634*, p. 315, Cambridge, 1840.

PALMER, W. M. *Camb. Antiquar. Soc. Communications*, 1911, xv, 208.

Roll Roy. Coll. Phys. of London, by W. MUNK, I, 158, London, 1878.

RALPH WINTERTON (1600–1636), M.D.

Regius Professor 1635–1636

Ralph Winterton shares with John Hatcher the shortest tenancy of the chair, namely for one year, death removing him from office in his thirty-seventh year, said to be that fatal to genius, and certainly at an age just thirty-three years less than the average age at death of the seventeen other Regius Professors of Physic. He was undoubtedly the most scholarly, and his literary style, not devoid of

1 Henry-André (*Les Ex Libris de Médecins et de Pharmaciens*, 1908), who includes Collins's book-plate 1634, describes as the first medical book-plate that in 1511 of Rabelais, dubbed "The Reverent Rabelais" by Sir John Harington in his *Metamorphosis of Ajax* (1596).

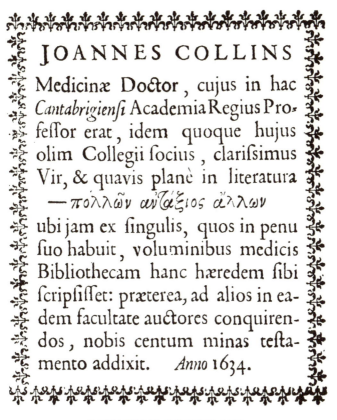

JOANNES COLLINS
Medicinæ Doctor, cujus in hac
Cantabrigienfi Academia Regius Pro-
feffor erat, idem quoque hujus
olim Collegii focius, clarifsimus
Vir, & quavis planè in literatura
— πολλῶν ἀν[ά]ξιος ἄλλων
ubi jam ex fingulis, quos in penu
fuo habuit, voluminibus medicis
Bibliothecam hanc hæredem fibi
fcripfiffet: præterea, ad alios in ea-
dem facultate auctores conquiren-
dos, nobis centum minas tefta-
mento addixit. *Anno* 1634.

DONATION-BOOKPLATE
For Professor John Collins's books left to St John's College

humour, recalls that of his longer-lived contemporary Sir Thomas Browne (1605–1682) of Norwich and the *Religio Medici*. Born at Lutterworth, Leicestershire, the son of Francis Winterton, he had a brother, John, who proceeded to the degree of M.B. in 1636. He went to Eton and then as a scholar to King's College on June 3, 1617, where he became a fellow on June 3, 1620, and proceeded to the degrees of B.A. (1620–1) and M.A. (1624). In 1625 he unsuccessfully contested the Regius Professorship of Greek against Robert Creighton or Critone or Crichton (1593–1672), fellow of Trinity, who held the chair until 1639 and in 1670 became Bishop of Bath and Wells. As a sufferer from melancholy and sleeplessness, Winterton consulted the then Regius Professor of Physic, John Collins, whose fatherly advice to "divert" from the study of mathematics to that of medicine was after some discussion granted by the college on August 20, 1629. In 1631 the death of his brother Francis in Silesia so much depressed him that he sought comfort in translating into English "The Considerations of Drexelius upon Eternitie" which, though dated King's College, June 1, 1632, was not published until 1636; eight subsequent editions came out between 1650 and 1724. It was dedicated to "The Right Worshipfull and truely religious Esquire, Mr Edw. Benlowes of Brent-Hall in Essex, R. W. wisheth Internall, Externall and Eternall Happinesse". The "Epistle to the Reader" gives the following account of his adventures in search of sleep:

Being designated by the statutes of my private Colledge to the studie of Physick, in the first place I thought good to spend some time in Arithmetick as being a necessarie instrument and help in my

Profession: in which I made some progresse...But the knowledge of this cost me so deare that I was forced to leave the studie of it: for many nights together I was constrained against my will to practise numerals oftener than I would, telling the clock...and so I went into the Physick and Musick Schools imploring at one and the same time the help of Hippocrates and the Muses. For at that time I turned the first book of Hippocrates, his Aphorismes into Greek Verses...But though I found some rest, yet I did not sleep so soundly as at other times. So I left the Temple of Hippocrates and the Muses and betook my self into the Sancturie to learn of David, divine arithmetic, which consisteth in the due numbering of the days of this life by comparing them with the years of eternity; and so I fell upon translating this book of Eternity. And this I found by daily experience to be the best hypnoticon that ever I used; for it brought me to my rest better than if I had taken diacodion" [a syrup made from the heads of poppies].

In 1631 he received the University licence to practise Medicine (M.L.), and in September 1631 petitioned King's College to grant him the degree of M.D.; this, however, was refused, and not conferred by the Provost, Samuel Collins (1576–1651), who was also Regius Professor of Divinity (1617–1651), until 1633 and then only after the intervention of Archbishop Laud in a letter dated December 12, 1633. In explanation of Winterton's application to his college for the degree of M.D. it may be mentioned that until 1852 the scholars of King's College enjoyed exemption from the ordinary examination for the B.A. degree and from the *deposition* of the regent doctors and masters in the case of all the superior degrees. Although a musician as well as a scholar, Winterton did not live in harmony with his fellows; the college records show that he was punished in 1631 and again in 1633 for indecorous and rude conduct in the college hall; his unpopularity therefore must have accounted for the delay in his being granted the degree of M.D.

In 1633 he published the aphorisms of Hippocrates (*Hippocratis Magni Aphorismi Soluti et Metrici*) done into Greek verse by himself and into Latin verse by John Fryer (*obiit* 1563) also of King's and the first Cambridge graduate to be President of the Royal College of Physicians of London (1549–1551). To the translations are appended a long series of Latin or Greek epigrams in praise of Winterton's work from the pens of the Regius Professors of Physic at Cambridge and of Medicine at Oxford, the President of the Royal College of Physicians in London and seventeen of its fellows (fourteen being Cambridge and three Oxford men), Francis Glisson, his successor as Regius Professor, and many others, so that "no medical work at Cambridge has ever received so high a degree of academical commendation" (Norman Moore). It appears to have insured his appointment by the King as Regius Professor of Physic in 1635 in succession to John Collins. Of the five Regius Professorships at this time three were held by King's men, namely Samuel Collins (of Divinity from 1617 to 1651), Thomas Goad (of Civil Law from 1635 to 1666), and Winterton. In addition to Greek verses he brought out translations of "The Meditations" (1631), of which there were many editions, and of "A Golden Chaine of Divine Aphorismes" (1632), both by Johann Gerhard (1582–1637), protestant divine of Heidelberg, editions of Terence (1633) which reached a sixth edition in 1640, and of the Greek poem "De Situ Orbis" of Dionysius (1633). His edition of the

"Poetae Minores Graeci" (1635) with observations of his own on Hesiod, was dedicated to Archbishop Laud, but its intended further expansion was not accomplished. No medical observations can be traced to his fertile pen, and he was not a fellow of the Royal College of Physicians of London, though it may be anticipated that he would have been had he lived longer. Like its founder, Linacre, he was a scholar-physician, and was more eminent in the first than in the second capacity. As Regius Professor he was scrupulous in the discharge of his duties and took steps to prevent any attempts to circumvent the regulations then in force that the course for the M.D. degree was twelve years. He indeed, though most intimate with his predecessor John Collins, wrote a long letter on August 25, 1635, to Simeon Foxe, President of the Royal College of Physicians of London, saying that he had regretted to see "sometimes a minister, sometimes a serving man, sometimes an apothecary, often times a master of arts (whereof some have afterwards assumed holy orders) admitted to a licence to practise in physic or to be incorporated to a degree without giving any publique testimony of their learning and skill in the profession". He had refused to give two or three licences to practise, had declined to allow a Leyden Doctor to be incorporated at Cambridge without public testimony of his abilities, and would not countenance such irregularities. He also complained in this letter, reproduced by Goodall, that physicians were only called in to see desperate cases or moribund patients.

In addition to professorial and academic work he took a prominent part in the management of the college estates, and compiled a volume of information on this subject, which was often transcribed and was the model of similar compilations made by the bursars and others up till the early years of the last century.

His death occurred on September 13, 1636, and he was buried at the east end of King's Chapel. It is disappointing that there is not any portrait of this scholar-physician in King's College or in any of his works.

REFERENCES

GOODALL, C. *The Royal College of Physicians of London*, pp. 443–4, London, 1684.

Information from the Records of King's College, Cambridge, provided by John Saltmarsh.

LEIGH, A. AUSTEN. *King's College, University of Cambridge College Histories*, pp. 100–106, London, 1899.

MOORE, N. *Dictionary of National Biography*, XXI, 696–7, London, 1909.

FRANCIS GLISSON (1597–1677),
M.D., P.R.C.P., F.R.S.

Regius Professor 1636–1677

Francis Glisson was the second of the nine sons of William Glisson of Rampisham in Dorset, where he was born in 1597, and educated at the local school for seven years. Entering Gonville and Caius College as a pensioner on June 28, 1617, he graduated B.A. 1620–1, M.A. 1624. He was a scholar (1617–1624), fellow (1624–1634), lecturer on Greek (1625), and, though not in holy orders, dean (1629) of the college. Then, possibly as the result of Harvey's discovery of the circulation (1628), he turned to the physic line, becoming M.D. in 1634, a fellow of the Royal College of Physicians of London on September 30, 1635, and Regius Professor of Physic in 1636, a post which he held till his death. Harvey complained that no man over forty accepted his views at the time they were brought out, but Glisson, though approaching that age, supported the discovery of the circulation of the blood and influenced his pupil John Wallis (1616–1703), the famous mathematician, to maintain the Harveian discovery in a public dissertation. After 1640 he was somewhat of an absentee, practising for a time in Colchester, where he was at the time (1648) of its siege, and afterwards much in London; being a pronounced Presbyterian he probably found the intensely Royalist atmosphere of the University distasteful. In 1660 he petitioned the University for five arrears of stipend, apparently the years 1643–4 to 1648 when, living at Colchester, he was entirely absent (M. Foster); the Calendar of State Papers, Domestic, shows that on April 7, 1654, an order was made to pay him all the moneys owing to him as Regius Professor. When the first President (Viscount Brouncker) and Council of the Royal Society named in His Majesty's (Charles II) Charter of the Royal Society, dated April 22, 1663, proceeded, in virtue of the power given them by the Charter for two months, to declare on May 20, 1663, ninety-eight others to be fellows of the Society, Glisson was one of the nineteen medical men in the list. He did yeoman's service during the plague of London (1665), and, like Caius, was President of the Royal College of Physi-

Francisci Glissoni Ætat: *sua 68.* Med. D.ⁿⁱ Effigies.

PROFESSOR FRANCIS GLISSON
M.D., F.R.S., P.R.C.P.

cians of London (1667–1670), where he was also Anatomy Lecturer in 1639 ("De Morbis Partium"), Goulstonian Lecturer in 1640, Elect (1655), Censor (1656), and Councillor (1666 and 1670–1677).

Glisson was a philosopher, an anatomist, a physiologist, a good morbid anatomist, an orthopaedic surgeon, and a clinician. He described muscular irritability, proved that on contracting a muscle did not alter in bulk, and anticipated by almost a century modern teaching on muscular physiology in his *Tractatus de Naturâ Substantiae energeticae* (1672) and *De Ventriculo et Intestinis* (1677) published in the year of his death. His *Tractatus de Rachitide seu Morbo puerili* (1650), in 416 pages, is, except for Caius's *On the Sweating Sickness* which, though the classical account, is slight in comparison and lacking in the correlation of clinical manifestations and morbid changes shown in this treatise on rickets, the earliest monograph on a single disease published in this country. It was translated into English in 1651, and further editions in both Latin and English followed; described as "one of the glories of English Medicine", it was begun by a group of fellows of the College in 1645; the names of two of these (G. Bate and A. Regemorter) appeared on the title-page, but it was mainly Glisson's work. It was preceded by two publications on the same subject: Daniel Whistler (1619–1684), who was President of the Royal College of Physicians of London in 1683, read as his *Disputatio Medica Inauguralis* at Leyden in 1645 "De Morbo puerili Anglorum quem patrio idiomate indigenae vocant The Rickets"; this tract of eighteen pages suggested for the disease the truly formidable name "paedosteosplanchocaces". Although it has been stated that Whistler, knowing of Glisson's work, plagiarized it (N. Moore), there does not appear to be any evidence of this (Still). Arnold Boot (1606–1650), in his *Observationes medicae de Affectibus omissis*, written in 1645 but not published until 1649, included a chapter on rickets which he headed "De Tabe pectorea". Comparatively little was added to the knowledge of rickets until this century with the advent of vitamins and the influence of sunlight. Glisson's famous *Anatomia hepatis* (1654) has made his name and "capsule" familiar to generations of students. A keen clinician, his mental bent was directed even more to the elucidation of morbid changes and etiology.

His portrait at the age of seventy-five by W. Faithorne is in the Royal College of Physicians of London, the painter's engraving of which forms, with Glisson's arms— sable on a bend argent three mullets, pierced, gules, with a crescent for difference—the frontispiece of his *Tractatus de Naturâ Substantiae energeticae*. For the last two years of his life he had a deputy—Robert Brady, his successor— for the professorial work. He died at his house in New Street, Shoe Lane, London, on 14 October, 1677, and was buried in his parish churchyard, St Bride's, Fleet Street. His will, proved by his brother Paul Glisson on November 27, 1677, contained bequests to Gonville and Caius College and to Trinity Hall.

REFERENCES

FOSTER, M. *History of Physiology during the Sixteenth, Seventeenth, and Eighteenth Centuries*, pp. 284–296, Cambridge University Press, reprinted 1924.

LITTLE, E. MUIRHEAD. "Glisson as an Orthopaedic Surgeon", *Proc. Roy. Soc. Med.* London, 1925–6, XIX (Sect. Hist. Med.), 111–22.

MOORE, N. "History of the First Treatise on Rickets", *St Barth. Hosp. Rep.* London, 1884, XX, 71–82.

Roll Roy. Coll. Phys. of London, by W. MUNK, I, 218–221, London, 1878.

STILL, G. F. *The History of Paediatrics,* p. 209, Oxford University Press, 1931.

ROBERT BRADY (1627–1700), M.D., F.R.C.P.

Regius Professor 1677–1700

Robert Brady, the son of Thomas Brady (*obiit* 1671), an attorney-at-law of Denver, Norfolk, and Ann Brady, entered Gonville and Caius College as a sizar on February 20, 1643–4, was a scholar from 1644 to 1650, proceeded B.A. (1647–8) and M.B. (1653), and on September 5, 1660, was created M.D. by Royal mandate. He was a man of many offices for, being a strong Royalist, he was appointed the twenty-second Master of Gonville and Caius College on December 1, 1660, by Charles II's mandate, it being evident, according to J. Venn, that otherwise the fellows, of which he never was one, would not have chosen him. These circumstances were therefore the reverse of those attending the election of John Gostlin, the other Master who subsequently became Regius Professor of Physic. Soon after this, Brady was appointed Keeper of the Records in the Tower of London. He was admitted a fellow of the Royal College of Physicians of London on November 12, 1680, was physician-in-ordinary to Charles II and James II, Regius Professor of Physic from 1677 to his death in 1700, and Member of Parliament for the University in the Parliaments of 1681 and 1685, being followed in 1689 by Sir Isaac Newton. It is therefore not surprising that, like Glisson, he was much in London. In 1688 he was one of the physicians testifying to the birth of Prince James Francis Edward Stuart, the "Old Pretender".

In 1681, being concerned about the way in which the degree of M.B. was obtained, he petitioned the King for greater stringency in the conditions of graduation in physic, and accordingly Physic and Law were placed on the same footing by a King's letter dated April 8, 1681. He is noteworthy for having prescribed "Jesuit's bark" (cinchona) for ague about 1660, five years after it was first introduced into England. Sir Robert Tabor, Talbor, or Talbot (1642?–1681), who became a Court physician and obtained a popular, though not a professional, reputation for his treatment of ague by a secret preparation of cinchona, was apprenticed to an apothecary called Dean, in Cambridge, being admitted a sizar for five years at St John's College on May 19, 1663. He became active in the administration of cinchona to patients with ague about the time that Brady was employing it, and acknowledged his indebtedness for information on the subject to a member of the University called Nott, probably the Rev. John Nott (1624–1702), elected a fellow of Trinity College in 1647. It is not unlikely, though evidence is wanting, that the stimulus came indirectly from Brady.

Brady is chiefly known for his historical works, namely "An Introduction to the Old English History Com-

PROFESSOR ROBERT BRADY

M.D., F.R.C.P.

prehended in Three Several Tracts", 1681 fol.; "A Compleat History of England from the first Entrance of the Romans until the End of the Reign of King Richard II", 3 vols. 1685–1700 fol.; "An Historical Treatise of Cities and Burghs or Boroughs", 1690, 2nd edit. 1704 fol.; and "An Inquiry into the Remarkable Instances of History and Parliamentary Records used by the Author (Stillingfleet) of the Unreasonableness of a new Separation", 1691, 4to. He was a laborious writer going to the original sources for his information; but, according to F. Shoberl,

The value of his history is greatly diminished, by the perpetual pains which he takes to render it subservient to a preconceived theory about the novelty of parliaments, and, in fact, to the support of arbitrary power. He was physician in ordinary to James II and had not breathed the contagious air of a court without being affected by its influence; for he strenuously endeavoured to make the knowledge of our constitutional antiquities, in which he was deeply versed, instrumental in promoting the despotic views of the Popish king.

His only certain medical publication is a brief letter dated December 30, 1679, to his friend Thomas Sydenham, included with a long reply in Sydenham's *Epistolae Responsoriae*, inquiring about his treatment of ague by cinchona and asking if rheumatic patients might not be equally benefited by gentler methods than the copious and frequent bleedings he recommended. An anonymous tract, *Novae Hypotheseos de Pulmonum Motu et Respirationis Usu Specimen*, 1671, has been ascribed to him but without convincing evidence.

Brady, whose wife Jean (*obiit* March 1679–80) was the first wife of a Master of Caius to live in college, died on

157

August 19, 1700, and was buried at Denver on August 21; a black marble slab on the floor of Denver Church bears an inscription setting forth his virtues, achievements, and his arms. To Caius College he left 186 acres of land, £500 to buy the two separate rectories of St Michael and St Peter at Easthall and Westhall (though there is now one church only—St Mary's) at Denver, and his large library. There is a portrait of him in the Master's Lodge, Gonville and Caius College, a water-colour copy of which was done by G. R. Harding. The accompanying print from a copper plate by Edward Harding in 1799 was kindly provided by Dr H. S. Wellcome.

REFERENCES

PEACHEY, G. C. Private communication.

SHOBERL, F. Rudolph Ackermann's *History of the University of Cambridge*, I, 105, London, 1815.

VENN, J. *Biographical History of Gonville and Caius* (1349–1901), 1901, III, 105–109.

—— *Caius College, University of Cambridge College Histories*, p. 144, London, 1901.

CHRISTOPHER GREEN (1651–1741), M.D.

Regius Professor 1700–1741

Christopher Green or Greene was the son of Christopher Green, the cook of Gonville and Caius College, and was baptized in St Botolph's Church on February 23, 1651–2. On December 13, 1667, when sixteen years of age, he was admitted to the scholars' table at Gonville and Caius and was a scholar from 1668 to Lady Day 1674, when he was elected a junior fellow, becoming a senior fellow by Royal mandate October 3, 1682. Many college offices were discharged by him; he was ethical lecturer in 1676 and from 1679 to 1681, bursar 1687, steward 1684 to 1686, lecturer on Greek 1688 and, like Glisson, dean 1682. In the *Ordo Senioritatis* 1671–2 he was ninth and proceeded to the degrees of B.A. then, M.A. in 1675, and M.D. in 1685.

He married on January 21, 1688–9, Susan Flack of Linton, and had a son Christopher who entered Emmanuel (1708–9), proceeded to the degrees of M.B. (1714) and M.D. (1717), and died in 1738.

He was appointed Regius Professor in 1700. In November of the following year a legal decision involved the relations of the Royal College of Physicians of London with the Universities of Oxford and Cambridge; at the Guildhall the case of the College of Physicians against Henry Levett, D.M. Oxon., was tried before Sir John Holt, Lord Chief Justice of the King's Bench, and it was ruled that a graduate in physic of the Universities was liable to a penalty for practising in or within seven miles of London unless he had a licence from the College of Physicians. After a considerable interval, a Grace of the Senate on November 29, 1715, made a grant of fifty pounds to assist the doctors of physic graduates in resisting the College of Physicians; but in 1716–7 the court of King's Bench in the case of the College of Physicians versus Thomas West, D.M. Oxon., confirmed its ruling in 1701. In December 1721 the Royal College of Physicians of London addressed a letter in Latin to the Vice-Chancellors of Oxford and Cambridge urging them to be careful in admitting doctors in physic; this would suggest that Winterton's complaint to the College about the grant of the licence to practise physic (M.L.) in his predecessor's tenure of office was again justified. A reply, also in Latin, was received from the Public Orator at Cambridge undertaking to make degrees in medicine strictly conformable with the statutable qualifications; this appears to have been inspired by Green, for the Registry at Cambridge holds a receipt signed by him "for defending the privileges of the University against the College of Physicians". He was not a fellow of the Royal College of Physicians. When well advanced in years, he was probably glad to delegate his professional duties, for in July 1739 a revisionary grant of the chair was made to Russell Plumptre. William Heberden the elder (1710–1801) was then in Cambridge, and as Linacre lecturer (1734–1738) at St John's would have been a very suitable successor. His subsequent career in London naturally raises regret that he did not become Regius Professor, for, had he done so, he would probably have brought about a new birth of medicine in Cambridge more than a century before it actually did take place.

Green's portrait hangs in the hall of Gonville and Caius. He was described as "a very tall, thin, well-looking old man" (Cole). He died on April 1, 1741.

REFERENCE

VENN, J. *Biographical History of Gonville and Caius College* (1349–1897), I, 433, 1897.

Regius Professor 1741–1793

Russell Plumptre was born on January 4, 1709, in London, and came of a Nottinghamshire medical family, many members of which, including his nephew Robert Plumptre (1723–1788), President (1760–1788), were educated at Queens' College, Cambridge. His father, Henry (*obiit* 1746), a fellow of Queens' and of the Royal Society (1707), was President of the Royal College of Physicians of London (1740–1745), and his great-grandfather, Huntingdon Plumptre (1601–1660), of St John's College and Trinity Hall, was a successful physician at Nottingham and the author of *Epigrammaton Opusculum duobis Libellis distinctum* (1629). Russell Plumptre went to Eton in 1725 and was admitted a pensioner at Queens' College, Cambridge, on June 12, 1728, proceeded to the degrees of M.B. (1733) and M.D. (1738) but not B.A., was elected a fellow of the Royal College of Physicians of London on October 1, 1739, and in 1741 on the death of Christopher Green was appointed Regius Professor of Physic, having had a revisionary grant thereto dated July 1739. Like Haviland, he became Regius Professor at the early age of thirty-two years. In some topical verses on the Cambridge Commencement 1780, he is mentioned as the "gruff father of Physic". Addenbrooke's Hospital[1] was opened on September 29,

1 John Addenbrooke (1680–1719), M.D., a fellow of St Catharine's College, left about £4500 on the death of his widow, to trustees (the Master and fellows of St Catharine's) "to hire, fit up, purchase, or erect a building for a small physical hospital for poor people of any parish or county". Land was purchased in 1728, and a

1766, and for the first year he attended the patients, but his name does not appear among those of the staff in subsequent years. No publications, medical or other, can be traced to him. He died on October 15, 1793, at Cambridge, and was buried in Great St Mary's Church; he was described as having been for some years "the father of the University and the longest resident that had then been known". The last statement, however, shows the frailty of pious memories, for his immediate predecessor in the chair, Christopher Green, was a native of Cambridge and died there at the age of ninety years. Plumptre had one daughter, Mrs Ward, of Wilbraham, Cambs., who predeceased him.

REFERENCES

Gentleman's Magazine, 1793, LXIII, part II, 963.
Roll Roy. Coll. Physicians of London, by W. MUNK, II, 144, London, 1878.

building erected in 1740; but as the funds available were inadequate for its maintenance, an Act of Parliament was obtained in 1766 to make it a general hospital with a constitution under which additional funds should be obtained from voluntary contributions. The hospital opened with twenty beds. There is a historical resemblance between the origins of the hospitals at Oxford and Cambridge; the Radcliffe Infirmary, built on a site given by Thomas Rowley (1690–1758) and opened with thirty-six beds on October 18, 1770, received £4000 from the trustees of the will of John Radcliffe (1653–1714). In 1837 it had 144 beds. Addenbrooke's Hospital, which in 1834 contained sixty-five permanent beds, was largely rebuilt in 1864–5 from plans prepared by Sir George Murray Humphry and Sir Matthew Digby Wyatt (1820–1877), architect and first Slade Professor of Fine Art, Cambridge (1869–1873), and considerable additions have been made since, especially in 1913–1915 and in 1930. It had 200 beds in 1931, and when the new wings are completed will have nearly 300.

M.D., F.R.C.P.

Regius Professor of Physic 1794–1817

Isaac Pennington was born at Longmire in Furness Fell, Lancashire, in 1745, as the son of a captain of a merchantman—Paul Pennington. The association of the names Isaac and Pennington was familiar, for a Sir Isaac Penington or Pennington (1587?–1660), a puritan, was Lord Mayor of London, and his son Isaac was a prominent Quaker writer. But there does not appear to be any evidence that the Cambridge professor was their descendant. Educated at Sedburgh Grammar School, he entered as a sizar at St John's College on August 13, 1672, gaining a Lupton scholarship on November 4, 1766. In the Mathematical Tripos of 1767 he was thirteenth wrangler, five of the other thirteen wranglers being Johnians; one of the two moderators was Richard Watson (1737–1816), Professor of Chemistry from 1764 to 1773, when he was succeeded by Pennington in that chair. For about a year from November 3, 1766, Pennington was in charge of an observatory on the (Shrewsbury) tower over the gateway between the second and third courts of St John's with a salary of £15. He was elected a fellow on March 22, 1768, and, being admitted to a Faculty fellowship in Medicine on October 28, 1775, and remaining unmarried, retained this office for life. He held many College offices—Physical (Linacre) lecturer (1767–1817), steward (1774–5), junior bursar (1775–1787), bakehouse bursar and President (1787–1802). He proceeded to the degree of M.A. in 1770, and having entered at St George's Hospital, London, as a student in 1771, obtained the licence to practise (M.L.) in 1773, and became M.D. in 1775. Watson was elected Regius Professor of Divinity in 1771, but being unwilling to vacate the chair of chemistry, appointed a deputy; this gave rise to protests, and on December 15, 1773, Pennington was elected Professor of Chemistry after a hot contest (148 to 128 votes) with William Hodson (1743–1793), Fellow of Trinity, the affair being made one of rivalry between the two colleges, and held this office until 1794, when on 14 June he was admitted Regius Professor of Physic at the age of forty-nine. He followed Watson's example by having for a time a deputy, Isaac Milner (1750–1820), the first Jacksonian Professor of Natural Experimental Philosophy (1783–1792). He was thus a University professor for forty-four years, and held the Linacre Lectureship at St John's for fifty years; his tenure of professorial office, however, pales before the fifty-two years of his predecessor Russell Plumptre.

Elected physician to Addenbrooke's Hospital in 1785, he held office until his death. Two anecdotes of a rather different character are told of Pennington and Busick Harwood (1745–1813), who was Downing Professor of Medicine (1800–1813) and also Professor of Anatomy (1785–1813) at the same time. Pennington meeting his colleague one day greeted him with "Good morning Sir B-U-sick?" To which the other responded "Sir I-sic? I never was better in my life". The same play of words appears in the following lines about their playing duets together:

> Sir Busick, Sir Isaac,
> It would make you and I sick;
> Sir Isaac, Sir Busick,
> To list to your music.

PROFESSOR SIR ISAAC PENNINGTON
M.D., F.R.C.P.

In March 1794 Harwood quarrelled at Addenbrooke's Hospital with Pennington on the point whether or not the Regius Professor delegated his hospital duties, and sent the Regius Professor a challenge to a duel which, however, was received with contempt, the cartel not even being opened. The messenger, a Trinity undergraduate, posted off at once to town with this morsel of scandalous news which appeared next morning in the London newspapers. At the Royal College of Physicians of London Pennington was admitted a fellow on March 29, 1779, and in 1783 was the first Regius Professor of Physic to deliver the Harveian Oration, but it was not printed. On December 2, 1795, he was knighted at St James's Palace when the University presented a congratulatory address to George III on his escape from the recent attempt made on his life. Pennington was much interested in the movement of 1798 for national defence and took part in the volunteer movement of 1803, his colleagues as officers of the St John's College contingent in 1803, numbering forty-six as compared with forty-four from Trinity, being Lord Palmerston and Henry Martyn (1781–1812) the missionary. He does not appear to have made any published contributions to medicine. At the time of his death, February 3, 1817, he was the senior fellow of St John's.

In the dining room of the Master's Lodge of St John's College there is a portrait of him with a pleasing face and his own white hair; there is also a portrait labelled Sir Isaac Pennington and said to be by Sir Joshua Reynolds in the combination room of St John's, but its authenticity is open to considerable doubt. His commanding figure is well shown in R. Ackermann's *History of the University of Cambridge*, vol. II, in which J. Agar's tinted engraving of the "Doctor of Physic" is believed to be he: Sir Robert Scott, the Master of St John's, identified as representing him a caricature entitled "A Walk from Bridge Street to St John's Hall" (Richard Dighton, 1815). To W. L. Mansel (1753–1820), Master of Trinity (1798–1820) and maker of epigrams, is ascribed the following, which was subsequently done into Latin by B. H. Kennedy (1804–1889), Regius Professor of Greek (1867–1889):

> For female ills when Pennington indites,
> Not minding *what*, but only *how* he writes,
> The ladies, while his graceful form they scan,
> Cry with ill-omened rapture—*killing man.*

A tablet to his memory is in the ante-chapel of the college. Like Caius, he was unmarried and so was able to be a generous benefactor to his own college and to the University. To his old college he left money to endow exhibitions to candidates from Hawkshead and Colton, near his birthplace, and to the Master his landed property in St Sepulchre's parish, Cambridge, including his house, now 69 Bridge Street, in which a succession of medical men have lived for many years; the residue of his estate was left to St John's to pay £200 a year to the Master if he were also rector of Freshwater in the Isle of Wight, but if he were not rector of that parish the income was to be invested until he became rector, when he should receive £200 a year with the interest on the accumulations. These regulations as to the Master's income were annulled by the Statutes of 1856–1860.

To the University he gave in 1804 a small but choice

anatomical collection formed by Thomas Lawrence (1711–1783), Reader in Anatomy to the University of Oxford (1745–1750), President of the Royal College of Physicians of London (1767–1775), the friend of Samuel Johnson, and described as "so pious, learned, and skilful in his profession that the world was not worthy of him".

REFERENCE

Admissions to the College of St John the Evangelist in the University of Cambridge, part III, July 1715–November 1767, edited with notes by R. F. Scott, pp. 683–6, Cambridge, 1903.

JOHN   HAVILAND   (1785–1851),   M.D.,   F.R.C.P.
Regius Professor 1817–1851

John Haviland, the fifteenth Regius Professor of Physic, came of an old Norman family—the De Havillands—of Guernsey, who migrated to Dorsetshire in the fifteenth century and after that lived chiefly in Somersetshire. The future Professor was the only son of John Haviland, surgeon, of Gundenham Manor, Bridgwater, Somerset, and Mary, daughter and co-heiress of the Reverend S. Codrington Glover, vicar of St Mary's, Bridgwater. John was a family name; thus John Haviland (1792–1852) M.R.I.B.A., his contemporary relative, died at Philadelphia, Pa. Born on February 2, 1785, he was educated at Winchester for five years under Dr W. S. Goddard (1757–1845), one of its best head-masters (1796–1809), who probably inspired his pupil Thomas Arnold (1795–1842) with some of the educational principles set in force at Rugby, such as governing boys by reliance on their sense of honour. Admitted a pensioner at Gonville and Caius College on June 28, 1803, he was elected a scholar at Michaelmas in the same year, but three terms later migrated to St John's, where he was admitted a pensioner on October 13, 1804, and a scholar on the following 4th November. In January 1807 he was twelfth and last of the wranglers, the senior, third, fifth, sixth, and ninth being also Johnians. Esteemed as a good classic, he was said to have been remarkable for the elegant style in which he conducted the keeping of the medical Acts and in presenting candidates for degrees. As the Classical Tripos was not established until 1824, his name of course does not appear there. In 1810 he proceeded to the degree of M.A. and was elected to a fellowship at St John's, which he vacated on marrying on March 31, 1819, Louisa, younger daughter and co-heiress of the Rev. G. Pollen of Little Bookham Manor, Surrey. In 1807, after taking his degree, he began his medical education at Edinburgh, and after two sessions there spent three years at St Bartholomew's Hospital, London. Returning to Cambridge he took the licence to practise (M.L.) in 1812, and in 1814 was elected Professor of Anatomy (not human anatomy in particular) in the room of Busick Harwood (1745–1814), and gave the first regular course on human anatomy. Three years later, in 1817, he succeeded Pennington as Regius Professor of Physic, took the degree of M.D., and held the chair for thirty-four years until his death in 1851. The letters patent dated September 11, 1817, appointed him "Reader in the Science of Physic", the word Professor not being used.

PROFESSOR JOHN HAVILAND, M.D., F.R.C.P.

He was Linacre lecturer at St John's College for two periods, 1817–1821 and 1826–1847, Sir Thomas Watson (1792–1882) intervening. From 1817 to 1839 he was physician to Addenbrooke's Hospital, where in 1838 he contracted typhus fever followed by slight paralysis. He then retired from an extensive practice in the town and county, which had often obliged him to be on the road for forty-eight hours at a stretch, sleeping and eating in his carriage; this professional success and his private fortune enabled him to buy Ditton Hall and considerable property at Fen Ditton. He handed on a good deal of his professional work to his subsequent successor, Dr Bond. Elected a fellow of the Royal College of Physicians of London in 1818, he gave the Harveian Oration in 1837, which until 1864 was delivered in Latin. The Harveian Orator of the previous year (1836), who also refrained from printing his Oration, was his brother Regius of Oxford, John Kidd (1776–1851), who had previously been Professor of Chemistry and Lee's Reader in anatomy; by a coincidence the two Regii also died in the same year. Alike in these respects, they differed in their literary output; Kidd wrote several books, including the second of the Bridgewater treatises, *Adaptation of External Nature to the Physical Condition of Man* (1833), for which he received £1000. Haviland's published contributions were few, namely a "Synopsis of a Course of Lectures on Anatomy"; "Some Observations concerning the Fever which prevailed at Cambridge during the Spring of 1815", read at the Royal College of Physicians of London on May 15, 1815, and published in the last but one (1815, v, 381–399) volume of the College's *Medical Transactions* which became extinct in 1820; and "A Letter to the Members of the Senate on the Subject of the Subscriptions required of Medical Graduates in the University of Cambridge" (?1833), "subscriptions" meaning agreement with the articles of Religion. In the course of this letter it is stated that the Royal College of Physicians of London had applied for powers to grant medical degrees. History repeated itself in this respect in 1887 (*vide* p. 29).

In November 1819 when the Cambridge Philosophical Society was founded by the energy of Adam Sedgwick (1785–1873), Professor of Geology, and J. S. Henslow (1796–1861), Professor successively of Mineralogy and Botany, for "the purpose of promoting scientific inquiries", Haviland was vice-president, and subsequently became president (1823–1825). The latter office was also held by the three progenitors of the modern medical school of Cambridge, Paget (1855–1857), Humphry (1871–1873), and Foster (1884–1886). When the third meeting of the British Association was held in Cambridge in 1833, Haviland was president of the Committee on Anatomy and Physiology, the secretaries of which were Bond and Paget, his two successors in the Regius chair. In the following year he gave evidence before the Select Committee of the House of Commons appointed to inquire concerning medical education.

He was described as an excellent practical physician, directing his attention not so much to the niceties of diagnosis as to the minutiae of treatment in which he specially excelled and was extremely fertile. He was said to have declined the offer of a knighthood as not a sufficiently high honour for a Regius Professor. He died of apoplexy in Cambridge on January 7, 1851, and was buried at Ditton. One of his five sons, A. C. Haviland, put up a memorial window to his father in the new chapel of St John's College, opened in 1869.

The Medical School of Cambridge owes much more to him than is now realized. For he was the first, beginning in 1819, to give regular courses of fifty lectures annually in pathology and the practice of medicine, which were attended on an average by thirteen medical students, and to make the medical examinations a real test. On February 27, 1829, entirely as the result of his insistence and influence, the Senate passed a Grace which recast the medical curriculum and examinations, thus laying the foundations of the present system.

As he wrote little, and personal memories die comparatively young, Haviland's name is seldom mentioned now, but if the progress of the Medical School since his time be a monument to his saving grace, he could hardly have wished for a greater.

REFERENCES

Gentleman's Magazine, N.S. 1851, XXXV, 205.
Information from F. H. Haviland, M.D.
Roll Roy. Coll. Physicians of London, by W. MUNK, III, 183–5, London, 1878.

HENRY JOHN HAYLES BOND (1801–1883), M.D., F.R.C.P.

Regius Professor 1851–1872

Henry John Hayles Bond was born at Wheatacre, Norfolk, as the younger son of William Bond (1746–

1832), rector of the parish and a fellow of Gonville and Caius College, and shared his father's longevity. Educated at the Norwich Grammar School under Edward Valpy, he was admitted a pensioner at Corpus Christi, Cambridge, on July 7, 1819. He took the licence to practise physic (M.L.) in 1829 and proceeded to the degrees of M.B. (1825) and M.D. (1831), but did not take an Arts' degree or become a scholar or fellow of the College.

He studied medicine at Cambridge, Edinburgh, Paris, and in 1827 when a clinical clerk at St Bartholomew's Hospital, London, under Peter Mere Latham (1789–1875) was, with George Burrows (1801–1887), afterwards President (1871–1876) of the Royal College of Physicians of London, one of the first in this country to practise auscultation, his stethoscope being preserved in that hospital's museum. He settled in Cambridge and on October 4, 1830, was elected physician to Addenbrooke's Hospital, a post he held for nearly thirty-nine years, resigning on June 24, 1869. He practised at 56 Trumpington Street with much success but apparently without corresponding enjoyment; he was a sound physician and employed open-air methods in the treatment of pneumonia. A retiring man of sterling integrity, he was averse from personal advertisement, avoided the manners of a courtier, and was therefore sometimes regarded as being rather abrupt, but he was truly sincere, considerate, and kind-hearted. At the Royal College of Physicians of London he became a member in 1831, and a fellow four years later.

Appointed Regius Professor in 1851, he resigned on January 2, 1872, to live another eleven years, a some-

PROFESSOR H. J. H. BOND, M.D., F.R.C.P.

what unusual course, for the first two—Blyth and Hatcher—of his predecessors were the only others voluntarily to vacate the chair, Hatcher living for thirty-two years after this act. A conscientious teacher, he lectured regularly, but his only publication was *An Analysis of an Elementary Course on Pathology*, 8vo, London, 1866. When the General Council of Medical Education and Registration of the United Kingdom was instituted in 1858 he was the representative of the University, but did not take any active part in its proceedings and in 1863 was succeeded by George Paget.

He married a daughter of William Carpenter of Toft Marks, Norfolk, a niece of Rear-Admiral Sir Edward Berry, and had a large family. In June 1882 he sustained an impacted fracture of the neck of the femur which united so perfectly that doubt was thrown on this diagnosis. He was, however, practically confined to bed until his death on September 3, 1883, and at the necropsy evidence of the fracture was not forthcoming until a section of the bone was made.

Some official decisions of the Senate during his tenure of office may be mentioned: in December 1857 an ordinance was passed, to come into force when the next Regius Professor of Physic was appointed, namely that "The University shall have power to determine from time to time, by Grace of the Senate, the time for which the Professor is required to reside in the University in every year, such time not to exceed eighteen weeks". On May 13, 1861, at the request of Dr Bond it was agreed that an Assessor should be appointed annually to assist the Regius Professor in the Acts for the M.D. degree, and

that the Assessor, who must be a Doctor of Medicine of
the University, should receive five guineas from the
University chest for each Act.

REFERENCES

Lancet, 1883, ii, 483.
Information from the Rev. Sir E. C. Hoskyns, Bart., of Corpus
Christi College, and G. E. Wherry, M.Chir.

SIR GEORGE EDWARD PAGET (1809–1892), K.C.B., M.D., F.R.S.

Regius Professor 1872–1892

George Edward Paget was, like Sir Hans Sloane, Robert
Boyle, and his own son-in-law C. S. Roy (1854–1897), a
seventh son. Born on December 22, 1809, at Great
Yarmouth, Norfolk, then a very busy port on the East
Coast, he was the third son to reach maturity of the
seventeen children of Samuel Paget (1774–1857), shipowner and brewer, and Sarah Elizabeth Tolver (1778–
1843) of Chester, who were married on December 1,
1799. George and his famous brother James (1814–1899),
who rarely took any important step in life without consulting George, have been compared with William and
John Hunter. He was educated at Charterhouse (1824–
1827), where he was head boy in mathematics, and was
a schoolfellow of W. M. Thackeray (1811–1863) and
George Stovin Venables (1810–1888), a member of the
Cambridge Conversazione Society, more familiarly known
as the "Apostles", and a fellow of Jesus College, who
broke Thackeray's nose in a fight and is commonly, but
probably without foundation (Brookfield), supposed to

174

have been the original of "George Warrington" in *Pendennis*. His elder brother Arthur Coyte Paget (1808–1833) shared rooms in the Inner Temple with Thackeray and was the prototype of a character in *Esmond*. Entering Gonville and Caius College in October 1827 he was admitted a scholar at Michaelmas 1828, and was eighth wrangler in 1831, having just had his fifth attack of rheumatic fever before that ordeal. He was a fellow (1832–1851) and, like his predecessor Christopher Green, held many college offices, such as catechist (1834), bursar (1835–1838), steward (1839–1841), and registrar (1843). His election to a medical fellowship determined his future career, for previously he had not any inclination towards medicine; he began his professional work in Paris, and continued it at St Bartholomew's Hospital, London. He took the degree of M.B. in 1833, the licence to practise in 1836, being the last Regius Professor to hold it, and proceeded to M.D. in 1838, the year in which he delivered the Thruston Speech at Caius. For forty-five years (1839–1884) he was physician to Addenbrooke's Hospital, where his bust in marble, presented by his pupils in 1885, is in the downstairs corridor in company with that of his colleague George Murray Humphry (*vide* p. 66) who was surgeon to the hospital for fifty-two years (1842–1894). A replica of Paget's bust is in the Council Chamber of the General Medical Council in London. Paget, like Sydenham, believed that every disease had its specific remedy; he laid much stress on elegant prescriptions containing many ingredients. In 1842, during the Regius Professorship of Haviland, he was instrumental in initiating the clinical examination of patients in the final

M.B. examination; this was the first time that a regular clinical examination took place in the United Kingdom, and it has of course now become universal. Until he married in December 1851 and became the first occupant of 2 St Peter's Terrace, Paget lived in college; under the existing statutes he then vacated his fellowship at Caius, and but for this would probably have been elected Master of the College in the following year; in 1881 he was elected a professorial fellow under the then new University Statutes. In July 1851 he became Linacre lecturer at St John's College and was re-elected until 1872, when, on appointment as Regius Professor, he resigned and was succeeded by J. B. Bradbury (*vide* p. 210). During 1855–6 he was president of the Cambridge Philosophical Society, and in 1856 was elected a member of the first Council of the Senate under the Cambridge University Act of that year. In August 1864 for the first time in its existence the British Medical Association, then with a membership of 2400, held its thirty-second meeting with an attendance of over 200 in Cambridge, which then had a population of about 27,000. Paget was president and P. W. Latham, afterwards Downing Professor of Medicine (*vide* p. 208), secretary. The presidential address pointed out what the University had and had not done for medicine; admittedly the medical school was small and, if the reputation of a University is to be measured by the number of medical men it turns out, it must be confessed that Cambridge has fallen short of its duty; "but if the office of a University be rather to educate men into the capacity for pursuing any profession" and to maintain a high standard of knowledge in its medical graduates, then Cambridge had no reason to fear criticism. Paget, who in 1849 had printed a letter from William Harvey to Samuel Ward, Master of Sidney Sussex College, Cambridge (1609–1643), and on June 26 of the following year *A Notice of an unpublished Manuscript of William Harvey*, pp. 20, delivered on June 26, 1866, the Harveian Oration at the Royal College of Physicians of London, on the text of Harvey's exhortation "to search and study out the secrets of nature by way of experiment", in which, with the question "Is there nothing more that we may learn from Jenner's discovery?", he prophetically suggested the subsequent activities of immunology. Having represented the University on the General Council of Medical Education and Registration of the United Kingdom since November 1863, he in 1869 succeeded George Burrows (1801–1887), also a former fellow of Caius, as its president and held this office until 1874, his tenure thus falling far short of that of another Cambridge graduate, Donald MacAlister, who was president of that much criticized body from 1904.

As Regius Professor (1872–1892) he was a dignified figure and, save Glisson, more distinguished than any of his predecessors; his lectures contained much personal experience of local interest, such as remarkable instances of survival of people buried for many days in the snow near Cambridge in times that now seem very far off. He combined rapidity of decision with accuracy of judgment; he liked to explain, when asked to approve the title of a thesis, that he had once been obliged to refuse the proposition "That mother's milk is the best for infants" as he was incapable of bringing arguments against it. On December

19, 1885, he was created K.C.B. (civil). He was an honorary D.C.L. Oxford and Durham, LL.D. Edinburgh, and F.R.S. (1873). He was asked, but declined, to stand as M.P. for the University in 1887, and on November 17 of that year George Gabriel Stokes (1819–1903), who was President of the Royal Society (1885–1890), was elected. Paget was much interested in natural history and was one of the ten original members of the Ray Club (founded on March 11, 1837, and named after John Ray (1627–1705), "the father of natural history in this country" and a fellow of Trinity), in Cambridge, the object of which was "the cultivation of natural science by means of friendly intercourse and mutual instruction". It was a continuation of Professor J. S. Henslow's Friday evening Meetings begun in 1827, and has had among its members four presidents of the Royal Society, Stokes, J. J. Thomson, Rutherford, and Gowland Hopkins. He was also a member of "The Family", a dining club of Jacobean origin, at the dinners of which the health of "The Family over the Water" was originally drunk; he was elected in the place of a member who was alive at the time of the 1745 rising, and himself gave a jubilee dinner when he had been a member for fifty years. Paget married on December 11, 1851, Clara, youngest daughter of the Reverend Thomas Fardell, LL.D. Camb., vicar of Sutton in the Isle of Ely, and had ten children, three of whom died young. His three daughters married respectively J. J. Thomson, Master of Trinity, C. S. Roy, Professor of Pathology (1884–1897), and Hans F. Gadow (1855–1928), Lecturer (1884–1919) and Reader (1919–1928) in the advanced morphology of vertebrates.

PROFESSOR SIR GEORGE PAGET
K.C.B., M.D., F.R.S.

The latter part of the nineteenth century has been spoken of as the "golden era of Cambridge", and it certainly saw the phenomenal rise of its scientific and medical activities, the latter as the result of the influence of Paget, G. M. Humphry, and Michael Foster. Paget's share in the success of the Medical School has probably not been fully recognized; for in addition to being the quiet but moving force behind his two predecessors he was instrumental in establishing the Natural Sciences Tripos in 1848, the first examination being in 1851, and took an active part in the early examinations. Further, during his term of office the Diploma of Public Health was started in 1875, thus setting an example to the other Universities and examining bodies, and the professorships of physiology (1883), of surgery (1883, but discontinued since June 1921), and pathology (1883) were established.

His literary output was small by modern standards; his first publication was a paper on "Cases of Morbid Rhythmic Movements with Observations" in 1847 (*Edin. Med. and Surg. Journ.* 1847, LXVII, 60); in 1862 in a pamphlet "On the Proposal to introduce a new Grain Weight" he opposed the suggestion of the Pharmacopoeia Committee of the General Medical Council to employ the grain of the Apothecaries' weight. His Harveian Oration was printed, and he contributed reports on nervous cases to the medical press. The second of his four sons, C. E. Paget (1855–1927), Medical Officer of Health for the borough of Salford, brought out in 1893 a short memoir of his father with four previously unpublished lectures, including two on the causes of disease, namely alcohol and mental influences. Sir George died in Cambridge on January 29, 1892, of influenza. His portrait hangs in the hall of Gonville and Caius College, and in the college chapel there is a window to his memory showing St Luke, the beloved physician, St Nicholas, the patron saint of sailors, to represent his birthplace and love of the sea, and the miracle of healing at the pool of Siloam, given by Lady Thomson.

REFERENCES

BABINGTON, C. C. *The Cambridge Ray Club*, 1887.

BROOKFIELD, F. M. *The Cambridge "Apostles"*, London, 1906.

Information from Lady Thomson.

MOORE, N. *Dictionary of National Biography*, XV, 52, London, 1909.

VENN, J. *Caius College, University of Cambridge College Histories*, London, 1901.

RT. HON. SIR CLIFFORD ALLBUTT (1836–1925), K.C.B., M.D., F.R.S.

Regius Professor 1892–1925

Thomas Clifford Allbutt was the first Regius Professor who at the time of his appointment was not a resident in Cambridge, and was the last to hold the chair without any age limit of tenure. Born at Dewsbury in Yorkshire on July 20, 1836, he was the only son and elder of the two children of the Rev. Thomas Allbutt, vicar of Dewsbury from 1835 to 1862 and later rector of Debach-cum-Boulge and rural dean of Woodbridge, Suffolk. His mother was Marianne, daughter of Robert and Sarah Wooler of Dewsbury, her elder sisters being friends of Charlotte Brontë. Several of Clifford Allbutt's paternal uncles were medical men in the neighbourhood and he thus had access to their surgeries and copies of the *Lancet* when Thomas Wakley (1795–1862), founder and editor of that journal, was the pungent critic of the London Hospitals. In 1850 he went to St Peter's School, York, where it was said that there were boys better at classics and others better at mathematics than he, but none with such a good combined knowledge of both. Entering Gonville and Caius College on May 31, 1855, at a time when there were about half a dozen medical students in the University, he gained a Caian scholarship in classics on June 24 of the following year, and then read science. On June 28, 1859, he was awarded a Mickleburgh scholarship in chemistry which, with some increase in the emolument, he retained until Lady Day 1863. After taking the degree of B.A. in 1859, he was the only man in the first class of the Natural Sciences Tripos for 1860, gaining distinction in chemistry and geology.

Originally attracted to literature and art, the almost accidental reading of Auguste Comte's *Philosophie positive* decided him to adopt medicine as a career, and he worked at this subject at Cambridge under Paget and at St George's Hospital with Bence Jones (1814–1873) and J. W. Ogle (1824–1905). At that time surgery and obstetrics did not form part of the Cambridge examination for the M.B., and, as it was not considered etiquette for University men to compete for resident appointments at the London Hospitals, he was never a house-physician. While at St George's he came under the influence of Jacob A. Lockhart Clarke (1817–1880), the neurologist, and thus was prepared to appreciate the teaching of

B. G. A. Duchenne (1806–1875) (of Boulogne) when, after taking his M.B. in 1861, he spent some months in Paris and attended the clinics of Trousseau, Bazin, and Hardy. On returning to England he decided to practise as a consulting physician in Leeds, and in November 1861 was appointed physician to the Leeds Home of Recovery, which was a fever hospital. There in 1865–6 he treated, contrary to contemporary orthodoxy, the victims of a typhus fever epidemic by open-air methods with eminent success. In 1864 he was appointed physician to the Leeds General Infirmary and held this post until 1884.

In the early years of waiting for consulting practice at Leeds he utilized the time by reading and annotating widely, collecting and working up clinical material, and writing papers, especially in the *British and Foreign Medico-Chirurgical Review* and *St George's Hospital Reports*, both edited by his friend J. W. Ogle, who probably, like Hughlings Jackson (1835–1911), a fellow Yorkshireman, suggested the work which saw the light in his important monograph *The Use of the Ophthalmoscope in Diseases of the Nervous System and of the Kidneys, and also in certain General Disorders* (1871). He worked at the West Riding Asylum, of which J. Crichton-Browne was superintendent, and there collected much material for this epoch-making work and other papers of which there was a constant stream. As early as 1866 he introduced the present short form of clinical thermometer; as the previous instruments were about ten inches long and too cumbrous for ordinary use, the routine practice of taking temperatures was really made possible by Allbutt's invention. In 1868 he gave the first description of syphilitic disease of the cerebral vessels; as his article was hidden in *St George's Hospital Reports*, this important observation was often attributed to Heubner, who independently described the condition in 1873. In 1869 he advocated the hypodermic injection, a method then little known, of morphine in heart disease, and brought forward evidence of the water-borne origin of typhoid fever—a conclusion, like others he initiated, now merged in general knowledge. The following year saw the first of his pioneer papers on the effects of overwork and strain on the heart and great blood-vessels, the outcome of much careful clinical observation, and also a paper on tapping the pericardium, a result of Trousseau's teaching in Paris though practically unknown in this country. During these busy years he held various lectureships, on materia medica and therapeutics, comparative anatomy, and medicine; in 1871, being President of the Medical School, which celebrated its centenary in 1931, he gave the introductory address in October, dealing with the questions "What is disease?" and "Can we relieve it?" His second paper on the subject of strain of the heart and aorta appeared in 1873, and in the following year, on the retirement of a senior colleague, Charles Chadwick, he rapidly became the leading consultant in the area extending from the Trent to the Tees. He continued, however, to be active in clinical research, and in 1876 wrote a paper on mental anxiety as a cause of chronic renal disease, thus showing that he recognized the importance of the causes of chronic disease. In the following year he advocated the open-air treatment of pulmonary tuberculosis, a subject in which, as in all others he took up, he continued to be actively interested. In 1878, writing by invitation in the first number of *Brain*, he vigorously condemned the evils of brain-forcing in schools, and in his presidential address at the Leeds Philosophical and Literary Society on "The productive Career of Great Men" said that the age of greatest mental achievement was between forty-five and fifty. In 1880 he did signal service in initiating the practice of a preliminary consultation between medical witnesses in legal cases, and so obviated, at least in Leeds and Yorkshire, the scandal sometimes resulting from the divergent opinions given by expert witnesses. On June 3 of the same year he was elected a fellow of the Royal Society, an honour shared by two of his predecessors as Regius Professors of Physic—Glisson and Paget. In 1883 he was elected a fellow of the Royal College of Physicians of London, having taken the membership comparatively late in life in 1878, and on both occasions William Osler (1849–1919), his future colleague as Regius Professor of Medicine (1904–1919) at Oxford, was in the same list. His Goulstonian lectures on "Visceral Neuroses" at the College of Physicians in the following year exerted a salutary effect on the vagaries of the gynaecologists. The now established treatment of tuberculous glands in the neck was advocated by him in a short monograph in 1885 written in collaboration with T. Pridgin Teale (1831–1923). The calls of consulting practice were now crowding upon him, but in 1888 he delivered the address in medicine on "The Classification of Diseases by means of Comparative Nosology" at the Glasgow meeting of the British Medical Association, and, following the example of Sir Henry Acland at the Cam-

PROFESSOR THE RIGHT HON.
SIR THOMAS CLIFFORD ALLBUTT
K.C.B., M.D., F.R.S.

bridge Meeting of the same Association in 1880, began to urge the importance of comparative medicine and pathology which he often returned to, and in 1923 had the gratification of seeing an Institute for Research in the Pathology of Animal Diseases, and a professorship of animal pathology established in Cambridge. The strain of his professional work made him accept in 1889 a Commissionership in Lunacy, and he accordingly moved to London where he remained until 1892.

Shortly after Sir George Paget's death on January 29, 1892, Sir Andrew Clark (1826–1893), then President of the Royal College of Physicians of London and also of the Royal Medical and Chirurgical Society, was sounded on behalf of some members of the Medical Faculty by Alex Hill (1856–1929), Master of Downing (1888–1907), whether he would accept the chair. But he declined. Allbutt was then approached, after some hesitation agreed, was appointed on February 21, 1892, and soon after was elected a professorial fellow of Gonville and Caius College.

Allbutt's appointment was the first occasion on which a physician not already resident in Cambridge had become Regius Professor of Physic, and was followed by a state of affairs which was most anomalous and unfortunate; for eight years Allbutt was without any status in Addenbrooke's Hospital, and therefore was in the position of a professor of physiology without a laboratory. In March 1900 this was corrected by an agreement between the University and the hospital that the Regius Professor of Physic should be a physician to the hospital (*vide* p. 30). Allbutt utilized these facilities but, except during a period in the War, when the Medical Staff of Addenbrooke's was depleted, did not take charge of beds. Howard Marsh, Professor of Surgery from 1903 to 1915, never took charge of beds in the hospital though, like Allbutt, he had the use of the cases for teaching.

In 1893 Allbutt began to plan a *System of Medicine* to take the place of that brought out in five volumes by John Russell Reynolds (1828–1896) between 1866 and 1879. This was probably the greatest of the many services he rendered to British Medicine; the work in eight volumes came out between 1896 and 1899, and in spite of many other engagements and the inherent difficulties and delays due to the large team of contributors, was carried through in a relatively shorter time than the second edition of eleven volumes (1905–1911). Among his numerous contributions to medicine the best known are his conception of angina pectoris as due to disease of the first part of the aorta rather than to obstruction of the coronary arteries or degeneration of the heart muscle, which he first put forward in 1894, and his recognition of hyperpiesia or high blood-pressure without any causal disease of the kidneys or arteries, which he first set out in February 1895. To these subjects he frequently returned in published addresses. At this time he began the valuable service of steadying and directing lay opinion by letters to *The Times* on subjects of current discussion, such as the criminal responsibility of the insane (September 1895) and the state of the Royal Army Medical Corps (1904). In 1896 and onwards he took an active part in University questions, such as degrees for women, the needs of the medical Faculty, the establishment of a Diploma in

Tropical Medicine and Hygiene (1903). On St Luke's Day, October 18, 1900, he gave the Harveian Oration at the Royal College of Physicians of London and dealt with "Science and Medieval Thought", having on October 1 delivered the Introductory Address at the Middlesex Hospital on "Abstractions and Facts in Medicine", setting out, as he often did in similar addresses, and especially in his book *Notes on the Composition of Scientific Papers* (1904; 3rd edition, 1923) the need for an accurate use of words. He indeed was so constantly writing and speaking at meetings that reference can be made to a few only; in September 1904 at the Congress of Arts and Sciences in connection with the World's Fair and Exposition at St Louis, Missouri, he delivered an address on "The Historical Relations of Medicine and Surgery to the End of the Sixteenth Century", insisting on their artificial distinction. On October 3, 1905, he delivered an address on medical education which, like the St Louis address, was subsequently published in much expanded book form. In 1909 and 1910 he gave the FitzPatrick lectures at the Royal College of Physicians of London on "Greek Medicine in Rome", which together with other historical essays were published with much elaboration in 1921.

Allbutt took an active part as spokesman of the British Medical Association's Committee on the Insurance Act (1911), and when the Medical Research Committee (later Council) was set up in 1913 was an original member and served until 1916. In 1912 he was for the second time a member of a Home Office Departmental Committee on Workmen's Compensation, which had not such an extensive reference as the one he also served on in 1906. During the European War (1914–1918) he undertook much work, such as honorary Lieut.-Colonel Eastern Division R.A.M.C., regular duty at Addenbrooke's Hospital when the staff was much depleted, and consultant physician to the special hospital for soldiers invalided for disorders of the heart, which was first at Hampstead and later at Colchester. His great work on *Diseases of the Arteries, including Angina Pectoris*, in two volumes, on which he had long been engaged, came out in 1915 when he was in his eightieth year, thus recalling Morgagni (1682–1771) whose *De Sedibus et Causis Morborum* appeared when the author was in his seventy-ninth year. In 1918 he became president of the newly established Papworth Village Settlement for tuberculosis, in which Sims Woodhead also took an effective interest. This pioneer institution, situated about eleven miles from Cambridge, was organized by P. C. Varrier-Jones and struck out a new line, namely a colony where the recovered tuberculous patient could earn a living, which Allbutt strongly supported. In 1914 Allbutt had been elected President of the British Medical Association for the projected meeting in Cambridge in 1915; this was rendered impossible by the War, but he was President both at its Clinical and Scientific Meeting in London in April 1919, and at the postponed Meeting at Cambridge on June 30, and July 1 and 2, 1920, at both of which he gave introductory addresses. During the Cambridge meeting his portrait by William Orpen, subscribed for by the medical profession, was presented to him; it now hangs in the Fitzwilliam Museum. In 1923 he was the first president of the Section of Comparative Medicine at the Royal Society of Medicine and gave an introductory address on the "Integration of Medicine". He continued to be extraordinarily active in writing and giving addresses, and left behind him at his death a small work *Arteriosclerosis, a Summary View*, ready for the press.

Many honours were bestowed on him; in November, 1907, he was created K.C.B. (civil) and on July 5, 1920, a Privy Councillor; he received the Moxon medal for clinical medicine at the Royal College of Physicians of London in 1921, the gold medal "for distinguished merit" of the British Medical Association in 1922, the triennial gold medal of the West London Medico-Chirurgical Society in 1923, and numerous honorary degrees.

His death after some months of failing strength occurred suddenly on February 22, 1925.

REFERENCES

CLIFFORD ALLBUTT. *A Memoir*, London, 1929.
Brit. Med. Journ. 1925, i, 428–33.

IX. *John Caius* (1510–1573), M.D., P.R.C.P.

JOHN Caius, of whose name there were at least nine other forms (Cais, Cayus, Kaius, Kees, Keis, Kesse, Keys, Keyse, Keysse), was never a Regius Professor; but as the third founder in 1557 of the college which bears his name and in Fuller's words has been "a numerous nursery of eminent physicians", as President of the Royal College of Physicians of London for nine years in all, the pioneer of practical human anatomy in this country, and in Gesner's words "the most learned physician of his age", he was an outstanding figure in the history of the Medical School of Cambridge.

He was born at Norwich, probably in the parish of St Ethelred, on October 6, 1510, the son of Robert Caius (*obiit* 1532), a Yorkshireman, and Alice Wode or Woda, and after school education in his native town entered Gonville Hall on September 12, 1529, at the rather mature age, for that time, of nineteen. He was a scholar from Michaelmas 1530 to Lady Day 1533, and graduated B.A. in January 1532–3, being first in the *Ordo Senioritatis*, the equivalent of senior wrangler. On November 12, 1533, he was appointed the sixteenth warden or Principal of Physwick's Hostel,[1] an annexe of the college, bequeathed in 1393 by William Physwick, Esquire Bedell (1360) of

1 Fuller remarked that "Phiswick's Hostle, though worse than a Cambridge, was better than any Oxford Hall", and that "above four score commoners have lived at once in this hostle, repairing for prayers to Gonvil Chapel, and, if dying, interred therein". In Caius's time the Service was at 5 a.m. According to R. Parker

the University. On December 6, 1533, Caius was elected to a fellowship at Gonville Hall, which he retained until Michaelmas 1545. His main interest at this time was theological, as is shown by his translations of Nicephorus Callistus and Chrysostom, from Greek into Latin, a Latin paraphrase of St Jude by Erasmus into English, and an epitome of Erasmus's *Ratio Verae Theologiae*. In March 1539 he went to Padua and followed the clinical teaching of J. B. Montanus (1498–1552), living for eight months in the same house as Andreas Vesalius (1514–1564), who was then preparing his great work *De Fabricâ humani Corporis* (1543) and thus inspired Caius as an anatomist. On May 13, 1541, he received the diploma of Doctor ("artium et medicinae") at Padua, and for a year lectured in that University on the logic and philosophy of Aristotle concurrently with Realdus Columbus (1516–1559) the anatomist. Then leaving Padua in July 1543 he travelled in Italy, examining and collecting manuscripts of Hippocrates and Galen, and on his way home started a friendship with Conrad Gesner (1516–1565) of Zürich, a scientific encyclopaedist, "the German Pliny" and "the father of bibliography".

(*View of Cambridge*, translated by T. Hearne, p. 72, Cambridge, 1721) there were 400 commoners resident in the hostel. The hostels (*hospicia*) were at first boarding houses run as private ventures by Masters of Arts, and in pre-Reformation times the colleges stood in public estimation in much the same position as later did collegers to oppidans at Eton; the hostels died out after 1550 (J. Venn). H. P. Stokes (*Mediaeval Hostels of the University of Cambridge*, p. 57, Cambridge, 1924) gives a list of 136 such hostels; according to Caius there were seventeen hostels in existence in his time.

After his return to England in 1544, the year in which he brought out *De Medendi Methodo libri duo, ex Cl. Galeni et Baptistae Montani principium medicorum Sententia*, and translations into Latin of some works of Galen, he was probably for some time in Cambridge, but Venn could not find any evidence that, as is often stated, he practised there or in Norwich and Shrewsbury. It would, however, appear that he visited Shrewsbury in 1551 when the sweating sickness was raging there. For about twenty years, probably from 1546, he lectured on anatomy at the Barber-Surgeons' Hall in Monkwell Street, where the bodies of four executed criminals were made available for dissection annually by the charter of 1540; these were the first demonstrations of the kind in this country. On December 22, 1547, he was admitted a fellow of the Royal College of Physicians of London, and on March 30, 1550, was appointed an "elect" or one of the eight senior fellows who elected the President from amongst themselves, an *imperium in imperio* which ceased to exist in 1860. In 1551–2 he was a councillor, and was President 1555–1561, 1562–4, and in 1571. In 1552 he published the first account of a single disease in the vulgar tongue in this country, *A Boke or Counseill against the Disease commonly called the Sweate, or Sweatyng Sicknesse*; this short tract, written at the request of his friend Robert Warmington for the instruction of the public, he subsequently expanded and translated into Latin, *De Ephemerâ Britannicâ* (1556), thus no doubt conforming to the medical etiquette of the day. From 1551 until his death he rented for £4 a year a house in the parish of St Bartholomew-the-Less, now occupied by the pathological department of the Hospital, with which, however, he was never connected, and led a scholarly and somewhat solitary life. He was physician to three sovereigns, Edward VI, Mary, and Elizabeth, and was busily engaged not only in practice but in work for the College of Physicians, such as initiating and writing its annals from 1555 to 1572, and in planning his munificent endowment and expansion of his Cambridge College. The latter he first brought before the college authorities in 1557 without any hint that he was the intending benefactor; finding out that a charter of foundation was necessary, he obtained this on September 4 in the same year, being declared a co-founder with Edmund Gonville in 1348 and William Bateman[1] in 1353. With due ceremony on March 25, 1558, he handed over nearly all his wealth and landed property with a charter of foundation to the college, and on April 1 was created M.D. of the University. On January 24, 1558–9, he accepted election

---

1 William Bateman (1298?–1355), eighteenth Bishop of Norwich, his birthplace, from 1344, founded the "Hall of Holy Trinity" (Trinity Hall) for the study of Canon and Civil Law in 1350. He was the executor of Edmund Gonville, rector of Terrington and Rushworth in Norfolk, who on January 28, 1347–8, had obtained permission from Edward III to found a college, officially called the "Hall of the Annunciation of the Blessed Virgin", for twenty students in dialectics and other branches of science; it was originally on the site now occupied by Corpus Christi College. Gonville died in 1351 before his foundation was established; Bateman moved the college to its present position and altered the statutes so as to be more like those of Trinity Hall; on this account, and because of certain endowments, he became the second founder of what was commonly known as Gonville or Gunnell Hall.

as Master with prophetic reluctance, for he was prematurely aged, in feeble health, stern rather than genial, a *laudator temporis acti*, and out of sympathy with the militant puritanism, not to say vandalism, of the time which led to the wholesale destruction of works of art, embroidered vestments, and articles of virtu. In spite of his generous benefactions, such as all his emoluments from the time he became Master until 1566 for improvements in the college and a considerable sum for the Gate of Honour erected after his death, and the infinite trouble he took about the college and its statutes, his relations with the fellows of the college became strained; according to Venn the fellows were narrow- and bitter-minded, very young—none of them in 1564 being twenty-five years old—and Caius certainly expelled some of them. As President of the Royal College of Physicians he was necessarily much in London, and this may have had an adverse influence. The crisis came on December 13, 1572, when his rooms were systematically pillaged and the chapel ornaments, or "massing abominations" and "popishe trumpery",[1] as his enemies called them, were destroyed or burnt in the college court under the direction

1 The following note occurs on p. 42 of G. Peacock's *Observations on the Statutes of the University of Cambridge*, 1841: Caius "with a view to the probable restoration of popery had carefully preserved all the apparatus of the Roman Catholic service 'such as vestments, albes, tunicles, stoles, manicles, corporas cloths, with the pix and sindon, with the canopy, besides holy water stops, with sprinkles, pax censers, superalteries, tables of idols, mass books, port-cuisses and grailes, with such other stuff as might have furnished divers masters at one instant" (Strype's *Life of Matthew Parker*, book III, chapter IV).

of Thomas Bynge (*obiit* 1599), Master of Clare Hall and Vice-Chancellor, John Whitgift (1530?–1604), Master of Trinity and afterwards Archbishop of Canterbury, and Roger Goad (1538–1610), Provost of King's. After this Caius stayed in his London house, returning to Cambridge to resign at 6 a.m. on June 27, 1573, the Mastership in favour of Thomas Legge (1535–1607), also a native of Norwich, whom he brought from Jesus College, and to give directions about his own tomb in the college chapel. He died at his house in the parish of St Bartholomew's-the-Less on July 29, 1573, the day it was said he had predicted; when his body was brought to Cambridge "all degrees in the University met him in honourable manner, near Trumpington Ford and conducted him with the greatest funeral pomp to the College" (Parker) where he was buried with due solemnity in the chapel. Of the inscription, which he provided, "Vivit post funera Virtus. Fui Caius", it was said by Thomas Fuller "Few men might have had a longer, none ever had a shorter epitaph". The first four words of this inscription also appear at the end of the long epitaph on the memorial Caius erected in 1557 over Linacre's tomb in St Paul's Cathedral. Caius's grave was twice broken into during alterations, in 1719 and again in 1891 when Professor Alexander Macalister from measurement of the thigh bone estimated that his height was not more than 5 feet 1 inch. The monument originally over his tomb was moved in 1637, when the chapel was lengthened, to the extreme east end. There are four portraits of him in Gonville and Caius College.

Caius was much interested in symbolism, as is shown by the insignia he designed for the President of the Royal

College of Physicians of London, and his staff of silver, or caduceus, supported by four serpents to remind him, as Caius intended, "by its material (silver) to govern with patience and courtesy, and by its symbols (serpents) with judgment and wisdom". He also designed a caduceus with its cushion "of reverence" for his Cambridge college, and his own arms, two green serpents standing on their tails upon a green stone amid flowers of amaranth, signifying "wisdom stayed upon virtue and adorned with immortality", granted in 1560 by Laurence Dalton, Norroy King of Arms. He wrote much and upon very various subjects, his *De Libris propriis Liber* (1570) giving seventy-two titles; some of his works have already been mentioned, others are Latin versions of Hippocrates, his style being reminiscent of Celsus; *De Canibus Britannicis*, intended for his friend Conrad Gesner's *Historiae Animalium*, though not included on account of Gesner's death, was published in an expanded form by Caius in 1570. In the tract *De Pronunciatione Graecae et Latinae Linguae cum Scriptione nova Libellus*, based on observations made in 1544 but published posthumously only in 1574, he upheld the old pronunciation against the re-formed method introduced in Cambridge about 1539 by John Cheke (1514–1557) and Thomas Smith (1513–1577).

His *De Antiquitate Cantabrigiensis Academiae*, 1568, written under the *nom de plume* "Londinensis Author", concerns an interesting episode; when Queen Elizabeth visited Cambridge in August 1564 the Public Orator, William Masters (*obiit* 1590), stated that Cambridge was older than Oxford University, and this stimulated Thomas Caius (*obiit* 1572), Registrar and in 1561 Master of University College, Oxford, to write a reply, *Assertio Anti-quitatis Oxoniensis Academiae*, in 1564. John Caius, who was not any relation, seeing an unsigned manuscript copy, and instigated by Matthew Parker (1504–1575), Archbishop of Canterbury, countered with the anonymous publication mentioned above which is bound up with Thomas Caius's protest; he adopted the statements made previously by John Lydgate, Nicholas Cantalupe, and Polydore Vergil, that Cambridge was founded by one Canteber, son of the King of Spain and heir to the city of Cantebra in Spain, who being banished from his native land was hospitably received by Gurguntius Brabtruc, King of Britain, obtained the hand of his daughter Guenolena and with her the eastern part of Britain, and in 394 B.C. built a town on the river, called after himself Cante, later changed to Granta and to Cam—Cante-brigia, Cambridge. Caius thus went much further back than Sir Simonds D'Ewes (1602–1650), a fellow-commoner of St John's, the antiquary who, speaking in the House of Commons in 1642, was content to take it for granted that no one would dispute that Cambridge was a nursery of learning in the time of Alfred the Great five hundred years before there was a house at Oxford. The *De Antiquitate* was bound up with a further work of Caius, *Historiae Cantabrigiensis Academiae ab Urbe condita Libri duo*, edited by Matthew Parker (1574), on which Thomas Fuller drew considerably in his *History of the University of Cambridge from the Conquest to the year* 1634 (1655). His Annals of Gonville and Caius College, edited by J. Venn, were printed in 1904. He was thus one of the early Cambridge antiquaries.

REFERENCES

FULLER, T. *The History of the Worthies of England*, p. 276, London, 1662.

MOORE, N. *History of St Bartholomew's Hospital*, II, 416, London, 1918.

MULLINGER, J. B. "Caius" in *Dictionary of National Biography*, VIII, 221, London, 1886.

PARKER, R. *A View of Cambridge*, (1622), translated by T. HEARNE, p. 81, London, 1721.

Roll Roy. Coll. Physicians of London, by W. MUNK, I, 37–49, London, 1878.

VENN, J. *John Caius*, Cambridge, 1910.

—— *Biographical History of Gonville and Caius College* (1349–1901), III, 30–63, Cambridge, 1901.

X. *The Downing Chair of Medicine*

SIR George Downing (1684–1749), Bart., K.C.B., of Gamlingay, by his will dated December 20, 1717, left his property in Cambridgeshire, Bedfordshire, and Suffolk to trustees who in default of certain issue were directed to found Downing's (*sic*) College. His cousin Sir Jacob Garret (or Garrard) Downing, on whom the estates devolved, died without issue in 1764, and after more than thirty years' litigation the foundation of the college was recommended by the Privy Council on September 22, 1800. The college charter provided for two professorships—one of the Laws of England and the other of Medicine—as part of the college; these were filled up some years before the foundation stone of the college was laid on May 18, 1807.

On February 27, 1882, a Statute approved by the Queen in Council provided that the professor should receive from the University £300 more annually than the amount received as a fellow from Downing College, but not including his lodge in the college or any equivalent for it. Under the Statutes promulgated by the Royal Commission dated 1925 Downing College was relieved of any financial responsibility for future Downing Professors. The 1926 Statutes of Downing provide that, when the finances of the college permit, a Downing Reader in Medicine shall be appointed for three years by the Governing Body. The Downing Professorship of Medicine was abolished after the death of J. B. Bradbury (1841–1930), who held the chair for thirty-six years. The

199

office of assistant to the Downing Professor also came to an end, his duties having been "to assist the professor in the preparation of his lectures in pharmacology and therapeutics, in carrying on pharmacological researches, and in the management and care of the laboratory, and to give students such practical instruction and demonstrations in pharmacology as may be desired". The assistant had acted in this respect for some years under the Reader in pharmacology, and in view of the large number of students attending the classes in pharmacology during the Lent term and Long vacation it was important that these duties should be assigned to a permanent post, the holder of which should take part in research and teaching in pharmacy under the direction of the Reader. Accordingly Eric Holmes M.D., who had been assistant to the Downing Professor since 1926, was in 1931 appointed University Lecturer in Pharmacology as from October 1, 1930. A University lectureship on pharmacology, established by Grace of November 12, 1908, was abolished by Grace of May 16, 1919, when W. E. Dixon (1871–1931), was made Reader in Pharmacology by Grace of the same date.

For the last sixty years of the chair's existence the teaching of its occupants was concentrated on materia medica and therapeutics. There were five professors during a hundred and thirty years:

	Appointed
Sir Busick Harwood	1800
Cornwallis Hewett	1814
William Webster Fisher	1841
Peter Wallwork Latham	1874
John Buckley Bradbury	1894

PROFESSOR SIR BUSICK HARWOOD, M.D., F.R.S.

SIR BUSICK HARWOOD (1745–1814),
M.D., F.R.S.
Downing Professor 1800–1814, and
Professor of Anatomy 1785–1814

Sir Busick Harwood, the first Downing Professor of Medicine, was the second son of John Harwood of Newmarket, whose family had lived in that neighbourhood since the time of Charles II. After apprenticeship to an apothecary, with whom he disagreed, he went to London and obtained a surgeoncy in India where he amassed considerable wealth from attendance on native princes. Returning to England for reasons of health, he entered Christ's College as a fellow-commoner on September 22, 1779, and there lived extravagantly as a witty *bon vivant* whose conversation was "profligate and licentious in the extreme" (Gunning). He was much interested in blood transfusion, wrote his M.B. thesis (1785) on this subject the year after his election (March 27, 1784) to the fellowship of the Royal Society, and several times demonstrated this experiment on animals before crowded audiences in Cambridge. On the death of Charles Collignon in 1785 he was elected Professor of Anatomy and physician to Addenbrooke's Hospital; Henry Ainslie (1760–1834) of Pembroke College, who was senior wrangler in 1781 and afterwards physician to Addenbrooke's Hospital (1786–1788) and to St Thomas's Hospital, London (1795–1800), would have been a candidate for the chair of anatomy, but Harwood's friends brought on the election unexpectedly. The only other senior wrangler who took up medicine was Sir Donald MacAlister (*vide* p. 214).

After taking the licence to practise (M.L.) in 1787 Harwood proceeded to the degree of M.D. in 1790. By this time he had migrated to Emmanuel, then a Tory college with a parlour famous for hospitality, the ostensible reason being that he there obtained better rooms and a large garden; but it has been suggested that he was anxious by joining a Tory college to increase his chance of promotion, he having previously been a professed Whig (Gunning). The Master of Emmanuel, Richard Farmer (1735–1797), D.D., was a congenial spirit and appeared with Harwood in James Gillray's caricature "Matins at Downing College, Cambridge" (1810). In a letter dated October 12, 1782, W. L. Mansel (1753–1820), Master of Trinity (1798–1820) and Bishop of Bristol (1808–1820), wrote of him:

> To make men laugh as well as eat,
> The merry Master knew
> Was doubling the luxurious treat
> And heartier welcome too.

Harwood remained on friendly terms with Christ's and often dined there in vacations. In May 1798, three months before he married, he was made Captain of the armed "Patriotic Association of Cambridge Volunteers". Two years later he became Downing Professor of Medicine, but retained the anatomical chair until his death. He was also Vice-Master of Downing, and was knighted on June 11, 1806, at the Queen's Palace.

His habits and manners were rather remarkable; during his morning walk in term time he collected half a dozen guests for his 2 p.m. dinner and then not infrequently carved the turbot which had been dissected by his demonstrator, Orange, for the previous day's lecture, his guests almost always staying on for the lecture at 4 p.m. In 1792 there were riots in Cambridge and the Dissenters were regarded as enemies of the King; Harwood, who until a very short time before had professed to be a Whig, is credited with the following *obiter dictum*: "in general every man ought to be considered honest until he has proved himself a rogue; but with Dissenters the maxim should be reversed, and every Dissenter should be considered a rogue until he has proved himself to be an honest man". With W. L. Mansel he had a long-standing feud, possibly as rival wits, and, according to Gunning, they wrote obscene epigrams about each other. Stevens records the following incident: Mansel was at a breakfast party given by Harwood, who put an undergraduate nobleman at the same table as Mansel. The latter left abruptly, and next morning Harwood called at Trinity Lodge to inquire, saying to Mansel "I am come, my Lord, on the part of Lady Harwood and myself to ask—". Here the Master broke in "Sir Busick, I am a prelate of the Church, Heaven knows how unworthy—"; to which Harwood, as he fled, rejoined "Heaven does know, and so do I". The same authority describes how Harwood ingeniously arranged that a presentation of plate should be made to him and, when the subscription was limited to two guineas, anonymously sent a bank-note for fifty pounds. The episode of the challenge Harwood sent to Isaac Pennington is recorded elsewhere (*vide* p. 165).

He started the publication of a *System of Comparative Anatomy and Physiology*; but, as it did not receive sufficient support, one volume only—that on the organs of smell—appeared (1796); it was beautifully illustrated, original, learned, and was translated into German. He also gave the Downing Lectures: "A Course of Lectures on Domestic Medicine, calculated for the purpose of conveying useful information to those members of the University whose residence in the country may be so situated as to render it difficult or impossible to obtain advice in cases of emergency or danger". The synopsis dated 1807 ran to thirteen pages. In the same year he printed a synopsis of his lectures on comparative anatomy and physiology, and five years later dedicated to the Duke of Gloucester, Chancellor of the University, the synopsis of a course of lectures on the philosophy of natural history.

S. Harding was commissioned by him to paint small water-colour portraits of his University acquaintances which then decorated his walls; there were two of Harwood, one sitting, engraved by W. N. Gardiner and published by E. Harding in 1790, the other standing, engraved by J. Jones, and published in 1791 by S. Harding.

Having been connected with three colleges, Christ's, Emmanuel, and Downing, and holding two professorships, he died without issue in his lodge in Downing on November 10, 1814, and on November 15 was buried in a vault in the quadrangle close to the Master's Lodge and licensed by the Bishop of Ely, directly after Harwood's death, as part of the site of the intended chapel; lack of funds, however, prevented the college authorities, though they did their best, from fulfilling Harwood's anxious desire expressed both in his lifetime and in his will, to be buried in the chapel. After his death his anatomical collection was purchased by the University (*vide* p. 52).

REFERENCES

GUNNING, H. *Reminiscences of the University, Town and County of Cambridge*, II, 150, London, 1855.
PEILE, J. *Biographical History of Christ's College, Cambridge*, II, 310, 1913.
STEVENS, H. W. P. *Downing College, University of Cambridge College Histories*, London, 1899.

CORNWALLIS HEWETT (1787–1841),
M.D., F.R.C.P.

Downing Professor 1814–1841

Cornwallis Hewett was the son of William N. W. Hewett of Calcutta and later of Bilham House, near Doncaster, whose fortune suffered severely from his love of horse-racing. Sir Prescott Gardner Hewett (1812–1891), Bart., President (1876) of the Royal College of Surgeons of England and sergeant-surgeon to Queen Victoria (1884–1891), was Cornwallis's half-brother. Hewett was educated at Charterhouse, and entering Trinity College as a pensioner on October 18, 1804, graduated as the eighth junior optime in the Mathematical Tripos of 1809; he was elected a fellow of Downing in 1811, proceeded to the degree of M.A. in 1812, and taking the licence to practise (M.L.) on July 14, 1814, was elected Downing Professor in that year. He was tutor of Downing from 1820 to 1822.

Becoming M.D. in 1822, he was on August 19 admitted a member of the Royal College of Physicians of London, becoming a fellow on April 12, 1824. He was physician to St George's Hospital from March 25, 1825, to 1833, lived in Berkeley Street, and on January 20, 1832, was gazetted physician-extraordinary to King William IV. No published works appear under his name. His influence determined his more distinguished half-brother, Prescott, to enter St George's as a student in October 1834.

He died at Brighton on September 13, 1841.

REFERENCE

Roll Roy. Coll. Physicians of London, by W. MUNK, III, 280, London, 1878.

WILLIAM WEBSTER FISHER (1797–1874), M.D.
Downing Professor 1841–1874

William Webster Fisher was the son of John Fisher and was born at Thrimby in Westmorland. In 1825 he obtained the doctorate of medicine at Montpellier where he was on friendly terms with Auguste Comte (1798–1857), the founder of positivism. Then at the mature age of thirty he was admitted, on December 12, 1827, a pensioner at Trinity College where his elder brother, the Rev. John Hutton Fisher, was a fellow and assistant-tutor. Migrating in 1830 to Downing College, he graduated M.B. in 1834, was soon after elected a fellow, was bursar for twelve years, being followed in this office by John Perkins (1837–1901), LL.D., a well-known unconventional character, and was steward and librarian until his death. In 1841 he proceeded to the degree of M.D., and on November 3 of the same year was elected Downing Professor; in announcing his appointment *The Times* added the inspired comment that his politics were anything but conservative, and that he enjoyed a European reputation for his professional abilities. His first course of lectures starting on November 9, 1842, dealt with medical jurisprudence, and he subsequently lectured on various subjects, such as "the preservation of health", an "introduction to the study of medicine", but especially on materia medica and general therapeutics. It has been handed down from a pupil who formed one half of his class at a later date that his lectures were given in his breakfast room, and that often the class on "assembling" found the professor in bed and were directed to spend the interval, necessary before his appearance, in the examination of some ancient specimens (Gray). From 1868 his deputy (P. W. Latham) gave the lectures. He had a large practice and was physician to Addenbrooke's Hospital from 1845 to 1873. He is stated to have had poetical gifts, but the only literary effort listed in the catalogue of the University Library is "A Letter addressed to the Members of the Cambridge Horticultural Society on the subject of the fête given in the Grounds of Downing College in the year 1847". His death occurred in October 1874. His portrait hangs in the combination room of Downing College.

REFERENCES

GRAY, A. *An Episodal History of Cambridge*, p. 291, 1926.
STEVENS, H. W. P. *Downing College, University of Cambridge College Histories*, p. 145, London, 1899.

PETER WALLWORK LATHAM (1832–1923),

M.D., F.R.C.P.

Downing Professor 1874–1894

Peter Wallwork Latham was born on October 21, 1832, at Wigan as the eldest son of John Latham who was a medical man but was not related to the famous physicians, John (1761–1843) and Peter Mere Latham (1789–1875). After serving as apprentice to his father and continuing his medical education at Glasgow, he entered Gonville and Caius College in 1854, where in the following year he gained a scholarship and in 1858 went out as nineteenth wrangler in the Mathematical Tripos. In 1859 he was placed in the first class of the Natural Sciences Tripos with distinction in no less than five subjects, chemistry, physiology, physics, comparative anatomy, and botany, a record never equalled. After working at St Bartholomew's Hospital he was elected a fellow of Downing in 1860, and in 1862 assistant-physician to the Westminster Hospital. But in 1863 he returned to Cambridge as medical lecturer at Downing and physician to Addenbrooke's Hospital. In 1864 he proceeded to the degree of M.D. with a thesis on "The Early Symptoms and Treatment of Phthisis". From 1868 he acted as deputy for W. W. Fisher until in 1874 he succeeded him as Downing Professor and continued the lectures on materia medica and therapeutics. The Statute (*vide* p. 199) approved by the Queen in Council on February 27, 1882, concerning the emoluments of the Downing chair, gave rise to a discussion, lasting till 1884, between Latham and the University. This chair he held for twenty years and no more, as he had always declared was right, but he remained physician to Addenbrooke's Hospital until 1899. He enjoyed a large practice in and around Cambridge, and at the Royal College of Physicians of London gave the Croonian lectures (1886) and the Harveian Oration (1888), and was not only censor (1887, 1888) but senior censor (1894), a most unusual honour for a country fellow. Chemical theories attracted him, as was shown by his Croonian lectures on "Some Points in the Pathology of Rheumatism, Gout and Diabetes", which contained elaborate formulae and were considered to have impressed the authorities at the Royal College of Physicians of London in no small degree. No book of any size came from his active brain, but he wrote a number of papers in the medical journals, contributed to Quain's *Dictionary of Medicine*, and published a small work on *Nervous or Sick Headache* (1873).

Having lived in Cambridge for sixty years, Latham saw the phenomenal development of the Medical School under the stimulating influence of Paget, Humphry, and Michael Foster. With them, however, he did not act or see eye to eye, and seemed rather to enjoy than to avoid being in opposition; further, it was not until after his resignation in 1899 of the post of physician to Addenbrooke's Hospital that any arrangement was made between the University and Addenbrooke's Hospital whereby the Regius Professor of Physic should be *ex officio* a physician to the hospital. On G. M. Humphry's resignation as Representative of the University on the General Medical Council there was a contested election, an unusual event in this particular office; the poll on November 7, 1889, resulted in the election of Donald MacAlister, M.D., of St John's College, with 194 to Latham's 140 votes. He was twice married, in 1862 and in 1884; by his first wife, Jamima McDiamid, he had a son, Arthur Carlyle Latham (1867–1923), D.M., F.R.C.P., physician to St George's Hospital, who was specially interested in tuberculosis and active in the establishment of the Royal Society of Medicine in 1907. His second wife was Marianne Frances Bernard (1839–1926), Mistress of Girton (1875–1884); there was no issue of his second marriage. Remaining in Cambridge until 1912 Latham then removed to London; he died on October 29, 1923, at 15 Royal York Crescent, Clifton, Bristol, being then the senior fellow (elected 1866) of the Royal College of Physicians of London. The funeral took place at Canford Cemetery near Bristol on November 1.

REFERENCE

Brit. Med. Journ. 1923, ii, 902.

JOHN BUCKLEY BRADBURY (1841–1930), M.D., F.R.C.P.

Downing Professor 1894–1930

John Buckley Bradbury was born on February 27, 1841, at Saddleworth in Yorkshire, and was the eldest son of John Bradbury, merchant. After apprenticeship at the age of seventeen to a medical man, he entered Gonville and Caius College in April 1862, but migrated early in the following year to Downing on gaining a scholarship open to the University and tenable until the standing for the

M.A. degree if the holder obtained a first class in the tripos. In 1864 he secured the second place in the first class of the Natural Sciences Tripos, one of the examiners being P. W. Latham, his private tutor, future colleague at Addenbrooke's Hospital, and predecessor in the Downing chair. He then worked at King's College Hospital, London, returned to Cambridge in 1866 as assistant lecturer on medicine and natural science at Downing, and took the degrees of M.B. (1867), and M.D. (1870) with a thesis on vertigo which he published. After lecturing for ten years at Downing he taught anatomy and physiology at Caius until 1880, and was Linacre lecturer at St John's from 1872 to 1894. He gave the address in Medicine on "Modern Scientific Medicine" when the British Medical Association met at Cambridge in 1880.

In January 1894 Latham resigned the Downing chair, and on March 8 Bradbury was appointed; he then proposed to lecture on pharmacology, therapeutics, and the practice of medicine, and applied for an assistant; in the following May C. R. Marshall, afterwards Regius Professor of Materia Medica (1910–1930) in the University of Aberdeen, was appointed, and was followed in October 1899 by W. E. Dixon, who in 1909 became University lecturer, and in 1919 Reader in Pharmacology, and for many years carried on the teaching and directed research in this subject, thus realizing the hope expressed in Bradbury's inaugural lecture on pharmacology and therapeutics in 1894 that there would be "an active school of pharmacology similar to the schools of physiology and pathology".

At the Royal College of Physicians of London Bradbury became a member in 1867 and a fellow in 1874, being, like Latham, the senior on the list at the time of his death, gave the Bradshaw lecture on "Some new Vaso-dilators" in 1895, and the Croonian lectures on "Some Points connected with Sleep, Sleeplessness, and Hypnotics" in 1899. To Allbutt's *System of Medicine* (1899 and 1910) he contributed an article on "Disorders of Sleep".

He was physician to Addenbrooke's Hospital for the remarkably long period of fifty years (1869–1919) and had an extensive practice, continuing to see patients until the onset of his fatal illness a week before his death on June 4, 1930. He was twice married, and left £77,000.

REFERENCE

Brit. Med. Journ. 1930, i, 1113.

XI. *The Linacre Lectureship in Physic*

THIS lectureship at St John's College, founded in 1524 by Thomas Linacre (1460–1524), is the oldest medical endowment in the University,[1] for it preceded the establishment of the Regius Professorship by sixteen years. It, however, never played the important part intended by the founder for reasons given elsewhere (*vide* p. 7) and is of historical interest only. The first lecturer appears to have been Christopher Jackson, who was buried in the old chapel on July 2, 1528, his death according to a brass erected to his memory in the new antechapel being "e sudore britañico" or due to the sweating sickness; the fourth of the five epidemics between 1486 and 1551 of the English sweating sickness, probably allied to influenza, occurred in 1528–9. On the other hand, T. Baker, the historian of St John's, and C. H. Hartshorne of St John's, rather ponderously described by Dibdin as "the young thorough-bred bibliomaniacal racer", both

1 The Linacre Lectureships are not the oldest medical endowment in the Kingdom. At the University of Aberdeen, founded in 1498 by William Elphinstone (1431–1514), Bishop of Aberdeen, the office of "Mediciner" or "Medicus" in King's College was established in 1505 with James Cumyne as its first occupant. This appears to be the oldest endowment for medical teaching in Great Britain. In 1700 William, ninth Earl of Marischal, founded a chair of Medicine in Marischal College, of which the King was Patron, at least as early as the appointment of the second professor, Matthew Mackaile, in 1717. The two chairs were united in 1717.

state that George Daye (1501?–1556), Public Orator in 1528, Master of St John's in 1537, and Provost of King's from 1538 to 1548, "studied physic in his younger days and was the first that ever held the Linacer lecture, being complimented by Caius on his skill in that Faculty". As Jackson held the lectureship for such a short time, Daye may have been the second Linacre lecturer, and if so, certainly the first occupant of it well known in the University, and that this is probable appears from the fact that Caius did not enter Gonville Hall until September 1529.

Among the lecturers up to 1907 were four Regius Professors of Physic: John Collins, Isaac Pennington, John Haviland, and George Paget. Three were afterwards Presidents of the Royal College of Physicians of London: William Baronsdale, Thomas Gisborne, and Thomas Watson. Henry Paman and Edward Stillingfleet, son of the Bishop of Worcester, were Professors of Physic at Gresham College, London; William Heberden the elder was called by Samuel Johnson "Ultimus Romanorum, the last of the learned physicians", and by Osler "the English Celsus". Edward Wilmot, who married the daughter of the great Richard Mead (1673–1754), was about the ninth medical man to be created a baronet. Sir Donald MacAlister of Tarbert was Principal and Vice-Chancellor (1907–1929) and has been Chancellor since 1929 of Glasgow University, and President of the General Medical Council since 1904. Of the forty-five Linacre lecturers, several of whom were appointed more than once, either continuously or with some other fellow of the College intervening (Allott, Paman, Brackenbury,

Haviland), twenty-three were medically qualified. There was not any injunction, as at Oxford, to go outside the college when there was not a fellow medically qualified for the lectureship, and accordingly nearly half the Linacre lecturers were not medical men. Twice only, and in the second half of the nineteenth century, was the Linacre Lectureship bestowed on any one not a member of the college, namely on George E. Paget and on J. B. Bradbury who lectured on morbid anatomy from 1873 to 1884. The list of the non-medical lecturers contains a number of distinguished names: Henry Briggs was Professor of Geometry at Gresham College, London (1596–1619) and then Savilian Professor of Astronomy at Oxford; Matthew Prior, the poet and diplomatist, was a "medical fellow" for life and Linacre lecturer from July 5, 1706, to July 7, 1710. Though it is doubtful if he ever lectured, he appears to have thought out reasons why not to do so, for his *Alma or the Progress of the Mind* (written about 1715) contains in its third canto the lines:

> how could I explain
> The various labyrinths of the brain!
> Surprise my readers whilst I tell them
> Of cerebrum and cerebellum!
> How could I play the commentator
> On dura and on pia mater!

Prior's portrait by Kneller is in the old Combination room of Trinity College. John Cleiveland, the cavalier poet, was described by Fuller as "a general artist, pure latinist, exquisite orator and eminent poet". Thomas Playfer was Lady Margaret Professor of Divinity; George Ashby and William Ludlam, both in holy orders, are noticed in the *Dictionary of National Biography* on account of their eminence as antiquaries. Among the forty-five lecturers there were eight fellows of the Royal Society, one first in the *Ordo Senioritatis* (Peter Foster, 1549–50) and one senior wrangler (Donald MacAlister, 1877).

LINACRE LECTURERS

1524? Christopher Jackson, B.A. 1523–4, Fellow 1525.

1528 ? George Daye.

1547 William Bill, B.A. 1532–3, Fellow 1535, Master 1546, D.D. 1547, Master of Trinity 1551, died 1561.

1550 Henry Eland or Ailand.

1555 Edward Raven, B.A. 1546–7, Fellow 1551, M.L. 1557, died 1558.

1557 Peter Foster, B.A. 1549–50, first in *Ordo Senioritatis*, Fellow 1552, University Preacher 1560.

1560 William Baronsdale or Barnsdale, B.A. 1554–5, Fellow 1556, M.D. 1568, F.R.C.P., President Roy. Coll. Phys. London, 1589–1600, died 1608.

1568 Thomas Randall, B.A. 1560–1, Fellow 1561, M.D. 1577, F.R.C.P. 1584, M.P. 1585 and 1592, Physician to the Queen's Household 1595, died January 1600–1.

1576 William Lakin or Lakyn, B.A. 1564–5, Fellow 1566, M.L. 1579, Proctor 1579–80, M.D. 1580.

1580 Robert Bouth or Booth, B.A. 1570–1, Fellow 1573, died 1606.

1588 Thomas Playfer or Playford (1561?–1609), B.A. 1579–80, Fellow 1584, D.D. 1596, Lady Margaret Professor of Divinity 1596–1609.

1592 Henry Briggs (1561–1630–1), B.A. 1581–2, Fellow 1588, first Professor of Geometry, Gresham College 1596–1620, first Savilian Professor of Astronomy, Oxford 1619–1631.

SIR THOMAS WATSON, BART.
M.D., F.R.S., P.R.C.P.

1596   Thomas Cooke, B.A. 1585–6, Fellow 1586, Proctor 1595–6.

1600   John Collins, *vide* p. 144.

1604   Robert Allott, B.A. 1595–6, Fellow 1599, M.L. 1606, M.D. 1608, died 1642.

1620   Robert Mason (1589–1662), B.A. 1609–10, Fellow 1610–1632, Proctor 1619–20, LL.D. 1628.

1624   Robert Allott.

1635   John Hay, B.A., incorporated from Edinburgh, Fellow 1634 by Royal mandate.

1642   John Cleveland or Cleiveland (1613–1658), B.A. 1631–2, then migrated from Christ's, Fellow 1634–1645 (ejected), cavalier poet; wrote elegy on Lawrence Chaderton (1536? –1640), the first Master of Emmanuel.

1644   John Bird, an "intruded" fellow on December 4, 1644; identity doubtful but probably an Oxford graduate.

1647   Robert Wadeson or Waydson, B.A. 1630–1, Fellow 1639, M.D. 1647, candidate Roy. Coll. Phys. London 1647.

1651   Edward Stoyte, B.A. 1640–1, Fellow 1642–3, Taxor 1648 (a University officer, with precedence after the Proctor, controlling Cambridge market), M.D. 1651.

1654   Henry Paman (1625–1695), B.A. 1646–7, Fellow 1647, Proctor 1656, M.D. 1658, Public Orator 1673–81, F.R.S. 1679, Professor of Physic, Gresham College, London 1679–1689, F.R.C.P. 1687, Harveian Orator 1688; correspondent of Thomas Sydenham.

1662   Pierce Brackenbury (1633–1692), B.A. 1654–5, Fellow 1656–1692, M.L. 1662, M.D. 1665.

1670   Henry Paman.

1674   Pierce Brackenbury.

1678   Henry Paman.

1691   Edward Stillingfleet (1660–1708), B.A. 1681–2, Fellow 1683, M.D. 1692, Professor of Physic, Gresham College, London 1698, F.R.S. 1688.

1695   Thomas Gardiner (1665–1705), B.A. 1685–6, Fellow 1688–1705.

        Lectureship vacant from 1703 to 1705.

1706 Matthew Prior (1664–1721), B.A. 1686–7, Fellow 1688–1721, F.R.S. 1698.

1710 Edmund Waller, B.A. 1701–2, Fellow 1705–1745, died 1745.

1716 Richard Wilkes (1691–1760), B.A. 1713–4, Fellow 1717–23; practised at Wolverhampton.

1720 Sir George Edward Wilmot (1693–1786), B.A. 1714–5, Fellow 1716–7, M.D. 1725, F.R.C.P. 1726, Harveian Orator 1735, F.R.S. 1730, Physician-General to the Army, Baronet 1759, Physician-in-Ordinary to George II and III.

1724 Lancelot Newton (1692–1734), B.A. 1713–4, Fellow 1716–1734, Taxor 1718–19, Registrary of University 1726–1734, LL.D. 1728.

1732 Henry Goddard (1707–1767), B.A. 1728–9, Fellow 1730–1735, M.D. 1753; practised at Foston, Yorkshire, benefactor to Addenbrooke's Hospital.

1734 William Heberden the elder (1710–1801), B.A. 1728–9, Fellow 1731–1752, M.D. 1739, F.R.C.P. 1746, Harveian Orator 1750, F.R.S. 1749; his *Commentarii de Morborum Historiâ et Curatione* were published in 1802.

1738 Thomas Clerke, B.A. 1733–4, Fellow 1735–1744, barrister.

1745 Samuel Hutchinson, B.A. 1741–2, Fellow 1743–1753.

1753 Thomas Gisborne (1726–1806), B.A. 1747–8, Fellow 1753–1806, F.R.C.P. 1759, President Roy. Coll. Phys. 1791, 1794, 1796–1803, F.R.S. 1758, Physician-in-Ordinary to the King 1794.

1757 John Cam, B.A. 1753, Fellow 1754–1763; practised at Hereford, died 1809.

1763 George Ashby (1724–1808), B.A. 1744–5, Fellow 1748, President 1767–1775, B.D. 1756, antiquary.

1767 William Ludlam, B.A. 1738–9, Fellow 1744–1769, B.D. 1749, mathematician and theologian, died 1786.

1767 Sir Isaac Pennington, *vide* p. 163.

1817 John Haviland, *vide* p. 167.

1822 Sir Thomas Watson (1792–1882), B.A. 1815, Fellow 1816–1825, L.M. 1822, M.D. 1825, Proctor 1823–4, F.R.C.P.

1826, President 1862–1867, Baronet 1866, F.R.S. 1859,
Physician-in-Ordinary to the Queen 1870; published
"Principles and Practice of Physic" 1843.

1826 John Haviland.

1847 Henry Thompson (1815–1897), B.A. 1838, 7th classic,
Fellow 1842–1897, M.D. 1853, F.R.C.P. 1858, Assistant-
Physician Middlesex Hospital 1855, Physician 1859–1879.
A careful physician, said to have "once prescribed half a
leech". A fine presence, known as "Jupiter Thompson".

1851 Sir George Paget, *vide* p. 174.

1872 John Buckley Bradbury, *vide* p. 210.

1894 Sir Donald MacAlister.

In 1908 a new arrangement was made whereby the
lectureship was held for one year only; it was decided
"to invite annually a man of mark to give a single lecture
on the same general plan as the Rede lectureship" in the
University, also founded in 1524. The honorarium is ten
guineas. The following list gives the lecturers under the
new dispensation and their subjects:

1908 Professor Sir William Osler, Bart., M.D., F.R.S. Thomas
Linacre.

1909 Sir Victor Horsley, C.B., F.R.S. The Motor Area of the
Brain.

1910 Sir Patrick Manson, G.C.M.G., M.D., F.R.S. Lecture not
given on account of illness.

1912 Sir Ronald Ross, K.C.B., K.C.M.G., F.R.S. Recent Work
on Malaria.

1913 Sir Norman Moore, Bart. The Physician in English History.

1914 Professor Right Hon. Sir T. Clifford Allbutt, K.C.B.,
F.R.S. Public Medicine and Hospitals in Ancient Greece
and Rome.

1915 Professor E. H. Starling, C.M.G., M.D., F.R.S. The
Governor Mechanism of the Heart.

1916–19 No lectures.

1920 Sir Henry Head, M.D., F.R.S. Aphasia and Kindred Disorders of Speech.

1921 Sir Thomas Lewis, C.B.E., M.D., F.R.S. The Law of Cardiac Muscle with special reference to Conduction in the Mammalian Heart.

1922 Sir Humphry Rolleston, K.C.B., M.D. Some Medical Aspects of Old Age.

1923 Professor Sir Archibald E. Garrod, K.C.M.G., D.M., F.R.S. Glimpses of the Higher Medicine.

1924 Professor Sir Charles Sherrington, O.M., G.B.E., P.R.S. Problems of Muscular Receptivity.

1925 Lieut.-Gen. Sir W. B. Leishman, K.C.B., K.C.M.G., F.R.S. Health in the Tropics.

1926 Sir F. W. Andrewes, D.M., F.R.S. Diseases in the Light of Evolution.

1927 J. A. Murray, M.D., F.R.S. Multiple New Growths.

1928 Sir George Newman, K.C.B., M.D. Linacre's Influence on English Medicine.

1929 Peyton Rous, M.D. The Modern Dance of Death.

1930 Professor W. B. Cannon, C.B., M.D. The Autonomic Nervous System.

1931 Sir John Rose Bradford, Bart., K.C.M.G., C.B., C.B.E., M.D., F.R.S. Physiology and Medicine.

REFERENCES

BAKER, T. *History of the College of St John the Evangelist, Cambridge*, edited by J. E. B. MAYOR, I, 112, London, 1869.

HARTSHORNE, C. H. *Book Rarities in the University of Cambridge*, pp. 327–8, footnote, London, 1829.

JOHNSON, J. N. *Life of Thomas Linacre*, p. 276, London, 1835.

OSLER, W. *Thomas Linacre*, Cambridge, 1908.

SCOTT, R. F. Much personal help.

VENN, J. and J. A. *Alumni Cantabrigienses*, part I, from the Earliest Times to 1900, in 4 volumes, Cambridge, 1922–1927.

XII. *The Chair of Surgery*

IN 1878 the Board of Medical Studies addressed a communication to the Studies Syndicate unanimously recommending the establishment of a professorship of surgery, but this did not have any effect until 1883 when this recommendation was repeated and Humphry volunteered to take the chair without any stipend (*vide* p. 72). The chair was established by Grace of May 10, 1883, and Humphry was elected on June 20. After his death in 1896 the professorship was suspended until it was re-established by Grace of the Senate, June 18, 1903, when Howard Marsh was appointed with a stipend of £600 a year; he held it until his death in 1915. No further appointment to the chair was made, and it was discontinued by Grace of June 4, 1921.

REFERENCE

CLARK, J. W. *Emoluments of the University of Cambridge*, p. 250, Cambridge, 1904.

FREDERICK HOWARD MARSH (1839–1915)
Professor of Surgery 1903–1915

Frederick Howard Marsh was born on March 7, 1839, as the third child and second son of Edward Brunning Marsh, a farmer of Homersfield, on the Waveney, Suffolk, and Maria Haward of Brook, near Norwich.

Originally called Haward, he changed this to Howard. In 1856 he was apprenticed to his uncle John Marsh, a practitioner in St John Street, Clerkenwell, and in October 1858 entered the Medical School of St Bartholomew's Hospital. Qualifying in 1861, he was for two periods between 1865 and 1870 private assistant to his fellow-countyman Sir James Paget. Appointed assistant-surgeon to the Hospital for Sick Children, Great Ormond Street, in 1868 he became full surgeon there in 1879 and consulting surgeon in 1888. At St Bartholomew's Hospital, where he was elected assistant-surgeon in 1873, he did not become full surgeon until 1892 when he was fifty-three years of age. He edited Sir James Paget's *Clinical Essays and Lectures* in 1879 and wrote a number of papers mainly on the diseases of joints and children. At the Royal College of Surgeons he was an examiner in anatomy and surgery, subjects on which he had lectured at St Bartholomew's, and was vice-president in 1898 and 1901. Active at the old Clinical Society of London, he was its president in 1902, and was secretary (1885–1887) and vice-president (1891–1893) of the Royal Medical and Chirurgical Society, which in 1907 became the Royal Society of Medicine. He was a sound surgeon of the old school, a good anatomist, and a successful teacher of students. On July 27, 1903, a year before the end of his term as surgeon at St Bartholomew's Hospital, he was appointed Professor of Surgery at Cambridge, where in the following November he was elected a professorial fellow of King's College, settled down in Scroope Terrace, and in 1904 was made an honorary Master of Surgery. In 1907, on the resignation of Dr Alex Hill, he was elected Master of Downing College. In 1912 he became Sc.D. and also first Commissioner of Scouts in Cambridge and, taking the duties very seriously, began to fail in health within six months of the outbreak of the European War.

He died in Downing College Lodge on June 24, 1915.

REFERENCES

Memoir of Howard Marsh (with portrait), London, 1921.

PLARR'S *Lives of the Fellows of the Royal College of Surgeons of England*, II, 26–9, Bristol and London, 1930.

POWER, D'ARCY. *St. Barth. Hosp. Rep.* 1915, LI (with portrait).

Readership in Surgery. After Humphry's death, the chair of Surgery was suspended, and in its place a readership was established by a Grace, March 10, 1898. It was held by Joseph Griffiths of King's College from 1898 until it was suppressed by Grace, June 11, 1903, when the chair of Surgery was re-established.

A Lectureship in Surgery was established by Grace, December 6, 1883, and held by G. E. Wherry (1852–1928) of Downing College, until it was suppressed as from December 31, 1911, by Grace of January 18, 1912.

A Demonstratorship of Surgery was established by Grace of December 5, 1901, and filled by H. B. Roderick of Emmanuel, who held it until 1926, when he became a Faculty lecturer in this subject.

Index of Persons

Heavier type denotes the pages on which biographical details appear

Acland, Sir Henry W., 30, 54, 69, 184

Adami, John George, 25, 87, 88, 105, 111, 112

Addenbrooke, John, 161

Adrian, Edgar Douglas, 82

Ailand (*or* Eland), H., 216

Ainslie, Henry, 201

Aldrich, George, 54

Alexandra, Queen, 31

Allbutt, Rt. Hon. Sir Clifford, 30, 112, 121, 124, **180–189**, 219

Allen, Antony, 138

Allen, F. J., 55, 74, 90

Allott, Robert, 217

Anderson, Sir Hugh K., 33, 82, 92

Andrewes, Sir F. W., 220

Anningson, Bushell, 26

Arderne, John, 12

Aretaeus, 9, 23

Aristotle, 7, 191

Arnold, Thomas, 167

Ashby, George, 215, 218

Bacon, Thomas, 143

Baillie, Matthew, 65

Baker, Sir George, 18

Baker, T., 213

Balfour, F. M., 81, 87

Balfour, Lord, 33

Ball, W. W. R., 32

Banks, Robert, 49, **59–60**

Barclay-Smith, E., 32, 77

Barcroft, Joseph, 82, 83, 85

Barnes (*or* Barons), Robert, 6

Baronsdale, William, 214, 216

Barrow, Isaac, 142

Bartlett, F. C., 101

Bate, G., 153

Bateman, William, 193

Bayles, John, 48

Bazin, E. P. A., 182

Beckett, William, 49

Bentley, Richard, 16, 17, 79

Bernard, Claude, 88

Berry, Rear-Adm. Sir Edward, 173

Bill, William, 129, 216

Bird, John, 217

Blake, James, 48

Bloxham, Thomas, 3

Blyth, John, 121, 122, **128–130**, 133, 173

Boase, C. W., 3

Boerhaave, H., 18, 48

Bonaventure, Saint, 40

Bond, Henry John Hayles, 24, 102, 121, 122, **171–174**

Bonham, Thomas, 5

Boot, Arnold, 154

Bouth (*or* Booth), Robert, 216

Boyle, Hon. Robert, 9, 174

Brackenbury, Pierce, 217

Bradbury, John Buckley, 102, 176, 199, **210–212**, 215, 219

Bradford, Sir J. Rose, 84, 110, 220

Bradley, Richard, 17, 18

Brady, Robert, 12, 122, 125, **155–158**

Brandon, Charles and Henry, Dukes of Suffolk, 132

Branthwaite, William, 140, 143

Briggs, Henry, 215, 216

Briggs, William, 48

Brookfield, F. M., 174

Brouncker, Viscount, 152

Brown, J. J. Graham, 109

Brown, Thomas, 108

Browne, Sir Thomas, 147

Brunton, Sir Lauder, 87

Buckmaster, G. A., 111

Burdon-Sanderson, Sir John, 54, 87

Burrows, Sir George, 172, 177

Burton, William, 138, **139**

Buxton, Lord, 33

Buxton, J. B., 103
Bynge, Thomas, 195
Byron, Lord, 62

Caius, John, 8, 10, 22, 46, 47, 134, 135, 143, 166, **190-198**
Caius, Thomas, 197
Calanzuoli, 63
Cam, John, 218
Cannon, W. B., 220
Cantalupe, Nicholas, 197
Canteber, 197
Carleton, William, 75
Carpenter, William, 173
Chadwick, Charles, 183
Chaplin, Arnold, 24
Cheke, Sir John, 8, 128, 196
Clark, Sir Andrew, 185
Clark, John Willis, 65
Clark, W. G., 79
Clark, William, 50, 54, 62, **63-66**, 68
Clarke, Edward Daniel, 65
Clarke, J. A. Lockhart, 181
Clarke (Clarke-Whitfield), John, 65
Clerke, Thomas, 218
Cleveland (*or* Cleiveland), John, 215, 217
Clobery, Robert Glynn, 18, 122
Cobbett, Louis, 105, 111
Cole, William, 61
Collignon, Charles, **61-62**, 201
Collins, John, 47, **144-146**, 147, 150, 214, 217
Collins, Samuel, 148
Columbus, Realdus, 191
Comte, Auguste, 181, 206
Connaught, Prince Arthur of, 33, 80
Cooke, Robert, 125
Cooke, Thomas, 217
Copcot, John, 130
Crane, John, 123, 124
Creighton, Charles, 55
Creighton, Robert, 147
Crichton-Browne, Sir James, 182
Crooke, Helkiah, 144
Croone, William, 48
Crosse, John Green, 66
Cumyne, James, 213
Cuthbert, George, 49, 54, 56, **59**

Dale, Henry Hallett, 25, 82, 84

Dalton, Laurence, 196
Darwin, Francis, 26
Darwin, Sir Horace, 101
Davies, Richard, 14
Davy, Sir Humphry, 14
Dawson, John, 32
Daye, George, 214, 216
Dean, Henry Roy, 103, 107
Dell, William, 11
Dew-Smith, A. G., 82
D'Ewes, Sir Simonds, 197
Dixon, Walter Ernest, 200, 211
Downing, Sir George, 199
Downing, Sir J. G. 199
Drosier, W. H., 64
Drury, A. N., 84
Drysdale, J. H., 112
Du Bois-Reymond, E. H., 108
Duchenne, B. G. A., 182
Duckworth, W. L. H., 55, 61, 78
Duncan, Matthews, 111
Dunn, Sir William, 98
Durham, H. E., 111
Dyer, G., 20, 36

Edkins, J. S., 84
Edmonds, Thomas, 3
Edward VII, 31
Edwards, John, 15
Eichholz, A., 98
Eland (*or* Ailand), Henry, 216
Eliot, George, 79, 84
Elliott, Thomas Renton, 25, 84
Elphinstone, William, 213

Farmer, Richard, 202
Fisher, Rev. John Hutton, 206
Fisher, William Webster, **206-207**, 208
Fletcher, Sir Walter M., 25, 94
Foster, Sir Michael, 25, 26, 70, 72, 76, 78-83, **86-91**, 93, 95, 100, 112, 170, 179, 209
Foster, P., 216
Fox, Simeon, 150
Freville, Jane, 131
Fries (*or* Freis), James, 2
Fryer, John, 149
Fuller, T., 129, 143, 190, 195, 215

Gadow, Hans F., 178

Galen, 4, 7, 9, 11, 23
Gardiner, Thomas, 217
Garrod, Sir Archibald E., 220
Gaskell, Mrs E. C., 94
Gaskell, J. F., 97
Gaskell, Walter Holbrook, 26, 81, 93, **94–97**
Gates, Ernest H., 103
Gedge, Joseph, 83
Gerhard, Johann, 149
Gesner, Conrad, 191
Gibson, William, 49, 56, **60**
Gisborne, Thomas, 19, 214, 218
Glisson, Francis, 8, 47, 48, 124, 149, **151–155**, 177, 184
Glynn (Clobery), Robert, 18, 122
Goad, Roger, 195
Goad, T., 149
Goade, Thomas, 145,
Goddard, Henry, 218
Goddard, Jonathan, 9
Goddard, W. S., 167
Goltz, F. L., 108
Gonville, Edmund, 193
Goodall, C., 150
Goodrich, Thomas, 8
Gostlin, John, 122, 125, **140–143**, 155
Gower, Ronald, 73
Graham-Smith, G. S., 105, 111
Gray, A., 1, 207
Gray, Thomas, 122
Green, Christopher, 17, 121, **158–160**, 162, 175
Greenfield, W. S., 109, 114
Griffiths, Joseph, 72, 223
Gunning, H., 201, 202, 203

Hales, Stephen, 17, 58, 79
Hamilton, D. J., 114
Hankin, E. H., 84
Harding, E., 158, 204
Harding, G. R., 158
Harding, S., 204
Hardy, A., 182
Hardy, W. B., 81, 94, 111
Hare, A. W., 114
Harris, Thomas, 18
Harris, Walter, 18
Hartshorne, C. H., 213
Harvey, William, 8, 9, 144, 152, 177

Harwood, Sir Busick, 52, 62, 164, 165, **201–205**
Hatcher, John, 121, 122, **130–133**, 133, 142, 146, 173
Hatcher, Thomas, 131
Haughton, Samuel, 76
Havers, Clopton, 48
Haviland, A. C., 171
Haviland, F. H., 171
Haviland, John, 19, 20, 62, 65, 102, 121, 124, 161, **167–171**, 214, 218, 219
Hay, John, 217
Head, Sir Henry, 25, 220
Heberden, William, the elder, 18, 160, 214, 218
Heberden, William, the younger, 65
Henry VIII, 7
Henslow, J. S., 18, 170, 178
Herd, John, 136
Heubner, O., 183
Hewett, Cornwallis, **205–206**
Hewett, Sir Prescott Gardner, 205
Hill, A. C., 84
Hill, A. V., 82, 84
Hill, Alex, 76, 185, 222
Hippocrates, 9, 11, 23, 149
Hodson, William, 164
Holmes, Eric, 200
Homer, 12
Hope, W. H. St J., 125
Hope-Pinker, H. R., 74
Hopkins, Sir F. Gowland, 33, 82, 98, 178
Hopkins, William, 32
Horsley, Sir Victor, 219
Horton-Smith, Raymond John, 41
Hoskyns, Sir E. C, 174
Hugh de Balsham, 2
Huicke, Robert, 134
Humphry, Sir George Murray, 26, 27, 51, 53, 64, **66–74**, 78, 102, 162, 170, 175, 179, 209, 221
Humphry, William Gilson, 66
Hunter, John, 67, 71, 174
Hunter, William, 111
Hurry, Jamieson Boyd, 83
Hutchinson, Samuel, 60, 218
Huxley, Thomas Henry, 72, 79, 86, 88

Ingle, R. N., 26

Jackson, Christopher, 213, 214, 216
Jackson, Hughlings, 182
Jackson, Sir Thomas, 80
James, George, 6
Jebb, John, 31
Jenyns, Thomas, 49
Johanitius, 4
Jones, Bence, 181
Joyliffe, George, 48
Judaeus, Isaac, 4

Kanthack, Alfredo Antunes, **110–113**, 115
Keilin, D., 118
Keill, James, 48
Keinsham, George, 131
Kennedy, B. H., 166
Kidd, John, 169
Klein, E. E., 87

Lakin (or Lakyn), William, 216
Langley, John Newport, 26, 81, 82, 87, 89, **91–94**, 96, 98
Lankester, Sir Ray, 87, 88
Latham, Arthur Carlyle, 210
Latham, John, 208
Latham, Peter Mere, 67, 172, 208
Latham, Peter Wallwork, 31, 35, 65, 176, 207, **208–210**, 211
Laud, Archbishop, 148, 150
Lawrence, Thomas, 52, 53, 167
Lawrence, Sir William, 67
Lea, A. Sheridan, 26, 81, 92, 98
Leathes, J. B., 84
Lee, Matthew, 54
Legate, John, 125
Legge, Thomas, 140, 143, 195
Leishman, Sir W. B., 220
Lemster, 2
Lesturgeon, C., 64
Levett, Henry, 5, 159
Lewes, George Henry, 79
Lewis, Sir Thomas, 220
Linacre, Thomas, 5, 6, 150, 213
Lively, Edward, 135
Lockwood, C. B., 71
Lorkin, Thomas, 125, 131, **134–137**
Lower, Richard, 9
Lucas, Keith, 82

Ludlam, William, 215, 218
Ludwig, C., 95
Lydgate, John, 197

Macalister, Alexander, 11, 48, 52, 53, 58, 61, 72, **75–78**, 195
MacAlister, Sir Donald, 26, 177, 201, 209, 214, 216, 219
Macartney, James, 53, 63, 66, 77
McCrae, John, 88
McCurdy, J. T., 101
Mackaile, Matthew, 213
Mahomed, F. A., 70
Mansel, W. L., 166, 202, 203
Manson, Sir Patrick, 219
Marsh, Frederick Howard, 186, **221–223**
Marshall, C. R., 211
Martin, Henry Newell, 25, 79, 91
Martyn, Henry, 165
Martyn, John, 18
Martyn, Thomas, 18
Mason, Robert, 217
Masters, R., 58
Masters, William, 196
Mellanby, J., 84
Merton, Walter de, 2
Meye, William, 8
Miller, W. A., 72
Milner, Isaac, 164
Milton, John, 143
Mines, G. R., 82
Molteno, P. A., 118
Montanus, J. B., 191
Moore, Sir Norman, 72, 149, 154, 219
Moore, William, 143
Morgan, John, **58–59**
Mortlock, John, 131
Mountain, George, 141
Murray, J. A., 220
Myers, C. S., 100, 101

Newman, Sir George, 220
Newton, Alfred, 64
Newton, Sir Isaac, 8, 16
Newton, Lancelot, 218
Nicholls, A. G., 88
Nicolaus Salernitanus, 4
Nott, Rev. John, 156
Nuttall, George Henry Falkiner, 33, 117, 118

Ogle, J. W., 181, 182
Osler, Sir William, 30, 184, 214, 219
Owen, Sir Richard, 72

Packer, John, 142
Paget, Arthur Coyte, 175
Paget, C. E., 179
Paget, Sir George Edward, 67, 71, 74, 78, 121, 124, 170, **174-180**, 184, 209, 214, 215, 219
Paget, Sir James, 67, 174, 222
Paget, Sir William, 8
Palmerston, Lord, 165
Paman, Henry, 214, 217
Parker, Archbp. Matthew, 197
Peachey, G. C., 57, 58, 158
Peacock, G., 1, 14, 31, 194
Pennington, Sir Isaac, 17, 52, 124, **163-167**, 203, 214, 218
Perkins, John, 206
Perne, Andrew, 135
Perse, Stephen, 132
Petrie, Sir Flinders, 53
Petty, Sir William, 9
Philaretus, 4
Physwick, William, 191
Pickering, J. W., 84
Pinsent, Mrs, 101
Playfer (or Playford), Thomas, 215, 216
Plumptre, Henry, 161
Plumptre, Huntingdon, 161
Plumptre, Robert, 161
Plumptre, Russell, 17, 24, 121, 160, **161-162**
Powell, W. S., 31
Pretty, Miss Gwynaeth, 105
Prior, E. S., 30
Prior, Matthew, 215, 218
Protospatharius, Theophilus, 4

Quick, Frederick James, 117

Radcliffe, John, 162
Rainold, Thomas, 6
Rake, B., 111
Randall, Thomas, 216
Rashdall, H., 1, 120
Raven, Edward, 216
Ray, John, 178
Regemorter, A., 153

Reynolds, Sir J. Russell, 186
Ridley, Humphrey, 48
Ridley, Nicholas, 8
Rivers, W. H. R., 82, 100, 101
Roderick, H. B., 65, 223
Rolfe, George, 17, 49, **57-58**
Rolleston, George, 83
Rolleston, Sir Humphry Davy, 112, 127, 220
Ross, Sir Ronald, 219
Rous, Peyton, 220
Routh, E. J., 32
Rowley, Thomas, 162
Roy, Charles Smart, 26, 84, 102, **108-110**, 112, 115, 174, 178
Rushworth, John, 49
Rutherford, Lord, 178
Rutherford, William, 70, 87

Salernitanus, Nicolaus, 4
Saltmarsh, J., 138, 140, 151
Sandys, Edwin, 129
Schroeder van der Kolk, 53
Scotman, John, 60
Scott, Sir Robert, 166
Sedgwick, Adam (obiit 1873), 170
Sedgwick, Adam (obiit 1913), 26, 81
Seymour, Charles, Duke of Somerset, 12
Sharpey, William, 77, 86-88, 108
Sheild, A. Marmaduke, 55
Sherrington, Sir Charles S., 81, 82, 84, 87, 109, 220
Shipley, Sir A. E., 64
Shoberl, F., 157, 158
Shore, L. E., 91, 96
Sims, 68
Skeat, W. W., 128
Sloane, Sir Hans, 174
Smith, J. Lorrain, 105, 111
Smith, Sir Thomas, 8, 196
Somerset, Charles Seymour, Duke of, 12
Starling, E. H., 110, 219
Sterne, Laurence, 51, 61
Stephens, J. W. W., 111
Stewart, G. N., 84
Still, Geo. F., 154
Still, John, 130
Stillingfleet, Edward, 214, 217
Stokes, George Gabriel, 178

Stokes, H. P., 191
Stoyte, Edward, 217
Strangeways, T. S. P., 105, 111
Stukeley, William, 58
Suffolk, Dukes of, *see* Brandon
Sydenham, Thomas, 157, 175

Tabor (Talbor *or* Talbot), Sir Robert, 156
Tancred, Christopher, 22
Teale, T. Pridgin, 184
Thackeray, W. M., 174, 175
Theophilus Protospatharius, 4
Thompson, Henry, 219
Thomson, Sir Joseph J., 178
Thomson, Lady, 180
Thurnam, John, 53
Tomlins, Richard, 53
Trevelyan, G. M., 15
Trotter, Coutts, 79
Trousseau, A., 182
Tunstall, Cuthbert, 6
Turner, William (obiit 1568), 129
Turner, Sir William, 70, 76
Tyson, Edward, 48

Uffenbach, 10

Valpy, Edward, 172
Varrier-Jones, Sir P. C., 115, 188
Venables, George Stovin, 174
Venn, John, 100, 191, 192, 197
Vergil, Polydore, 197
Vernon, H. M., 84
Vesalius, Andreas, 191
Vigani, J. F., 17, 18
Vines, S. H., 81
Virchow, R., 108, 110

Wadeson (*or* Waydson), Robert, 217
Wakley, Thomas, 181
Walker, George, 134
Walker, Henry, **133–134**
Walker, John Lucas, 105

Walker, Rev. Richard, 132
Waller, Edmund, 218
Waller, John, 49
Wallis, John, 9, 152
Walter de Merton, 2
Ward, James, 100
Ward, William, 124, 136, **137–138**
Warmington, R., 192
Watson, Richard, 14, 48, 163, 164
Watson, Sir Thomas, 169, 214, 218
Webster, John, 11
Wellcome, H. S., 158
Wendye, Thomas, 8
West, Thomas, 5, 159
Westcott, F. B., 89
Wharton, Thomas, 48
Wherry, G. E., 26, 174, 223
Whewell, William, 21, 73
Whistler, D., 153
Whitgift, John, 46, 195
Wilkes, Richard, 218
Wilkins, John, 9
Willis, Robert Darling, 65
Willis, Thomas, 9
Wilmot, Sir George Edward, 214, 218
Wilson, James Thomas, 53, 56
Wilson, Sir Thomas, 141
Winstanley, D. A., 14, 16
Winston, Thomas, 48
Winterton, Ralph, 121, 124, 145, **146–151**, 160
Wolsey, Cardinal, 5
Woodhead, Sir German Sims, 103, 105, **113–116**
Woodhouse, John Thomas, 62
Wooldridge, L. C., 84
Wordsworth, C., 32
Wren, Sir Christopher, 9
Wright, Sir Almroth, 25, 105
Wundt, W., 100
Wyatt, Sir Matthew Digby, 162

Index of Subjects

Aberdeen University, early medical teaching at, 213

Addenbrooke's Hospital, 30, 69; and the Regius Professors of Physic and Surgery, 30, 165, 185; clinical instruction at, 27; foundation of, 161, 162

Ague, cinchona treatment of, 156, 157

Anatomical Society of Great Britain and Ireland, foundation of, 71

Anatomies, 11, 47, 48, 192; supply of bodies for, 51, 52

Anatomists, famous, 48

Anatomy Acts, 52

Anatomy, chair of, establishment of, 17, 47, 53; stipend, 54, 72; the Professors, 57–78; additional Professorship, 22

Anatomy, comparative, 50, 52–54, 63, 64; development of the study of, 47, 49; early teaching of, 49, 57, 190; Lectureships, Readerships, etc., 54, 55; microscopical, and the teaching of physiology, 77; scientific morphology and, 68; supply of bodies for, 51, 52, 57, 192

Anatomy, Department of, 47–55; the anatomical collection, 52, 63

Animal morphology, Lectureship in, established, 26

Animal pathology, 33, 103, 185

"Apostles," the Cambridge, 174

Arms, grant of, to the Regius Professors of Physic, 125, 136

Auscultation, early, 172

Bacteriology, early study of, 114

Biochemistry, Department of, 82, 98–99; the Sir William Dunn Professorship, 98; the Professorship established, 98; opening of, 33; Readerships, Lectureships and Demonstrators, 99

Biology, 50, 64; early instruction in, 81; growth of the study of, 89, 104, 117–118; pathology in relation to, 104; Quick Chair of, 117

Blood, circulation of the, 144, 152

Board of Medical Studies, establishment of, 23

Body-snatchers, 51, 59, 61

Book-plates, medical, 145, 146

Botany, establishment of chair of, 17; growth of the study of, 18; Lectureship in, 26

Boyle's "Invisible" College, 9

Brookes's Museum, 63

Caius College, foundation of, 193; insignia of, 196

Cambridge University, clinical study at, 21, 27, 104, 176; decadent state in eighteenth century, 14; early history of, 1; early inactivity regarding medical study, 7, 8; the "golden era" of, 179; government of, 15, 16, 20, 45–46; Natural Science Club of, 25, 26; number of medical graduates during 1500–1856, 24; resident members in sixteenth and seventeenth centuries, 10; Royal College of Physicians and graduates of, 5, 7, 10, 19, 29, 159, 160; Royal Commissions (1548, 1850 and 1919), 8, 21, 33; Statutes, see Statutes

"Caput", the, 15, 23

Chemical physiology, 33, 82, 98

Chemistry, establishment of chair of, 17

Cinchona, early use of, 156, 157

Circulation of the blood, 144, 152

Classics, dominating medical study in nineteenth century, 8

Clinical examinations, inception of, 176

Clinical instruction, 104; inadequate material for, 27; introduction of, 21

Clinical thermometer, introduction of, 182

231

Coaches, famous, 32
Coaching, private, 31, 32
Collective Investigation of Disease Committee, 70
Comparative anatomy, 50, 52, 53, 54, 63, 64; chair of, 64
Conjoint Examining Board of the Royal Colleges of Physicians and Surgeons, 40
Crane's Charity, 124

Degree of B.Chir., 24; number conferred in different years, 28, 29, 35; qualifications of candidates for, 28, 39
Degree of M.Chir., 24; establishment of, 24; number conferred at various periods, 25, 26, 34; qualification of candidate for, 42
Degree of M.B., clinical instruction for, 21, 27; curriculum for, 10; earliest granting of, 2, 3; improved examination for, 20; in absentiâ, 41; Natural Sciences Tripos in relation to, 26, 37, 38; number conferred in various periods, 4, 11, 21, 25, 26, 28, 29, 34; number of students entering for, 28, 31, 33; period of study for, 29, 31, 38; qualifications of candidates for, 28; subjects of the examinations, 25, 37–39; thesis for, 23, 39; women admitted to, 21, 42
Degree of M.D., ad eundem, 11; by Royal mandate, 12; Committee of Examiners for, 40, 41; curriculum for, 10; earliest granting of, 2, 3; honorary, 12; in absentiâ, 41; number conferred at various periods, 4, 11, 21, 25, 28, 34; qualification of candidates for, 3, 40, 41; subjects of examination for, 23; thesis for, 23, 40, 41; women admitted to, 42
Diploma, in Medical Radiology and Electrology, 44; in Psychological Medicine, 43; in Public Health, 43, 179; in Tropical Medicine and Hygiene, 43, 186
Dissections, 11, 38, 47, 192; supply of bodies for, 51, 52, 57, 61, 192
Downing Chair of Medicine, 199, 200

Downing Street Medical School, opening of, 30, 31
Drapers' Company, Physiological Department built and equipped by, 33, 80
Dublin University, 49
Dunn (Sir Wm.) Biochemical Department, 33, 98

Egyptian skulls and bones, 53
Electrology, Diploma in, 44
"Elects", Royal College of Physicians, 192
Embryology, early study in, 81; Lectureship in, 55
Examinations, for medical and surgical degrees, 37, 171, 175; improvement of, 20; women admitted to, 21, 34, 42; see also Degree
Experimental Psychology, chair of, established, 101; Department of, 100

"Family, The"—dining club, 178
Fellowships, 34
Foster (Sir Michael) Studentship in Physiology, 83

Gedge Prize in Physiology, 83
General Medical Council, 173; and period of medical study, 29; and registration of students, 28
George Henry Lewes Studentship, in Physiology, 84
Glasgow, the earliest Scottish University to confer the M.D., 3
"Glomery" schools, 1, 128
Gonville and Caius College, see Caius College
Grammar, schools of, 1, 128
Gresham College, 9
Gwynaeth Pretty Research Fund and Studentship, 105

Harveian discovery of the circulation, 144, 152
Histology, origin of the word, 89
Honorary degrees, 12
Horton-Smith Prize, 41
Hostels, 190, 191

Huddersfield Lectureship in Special Pathology, 105
"Humphryology", 73
Humphry's Hostel for Medical Students, 69

Immunology, 177
International Catalogue of Scientific Papers, 90
Italian Universities, medical activity at, 2, 6

"Jesuit's bark", early use of, 156, 157
John Lucas Walker Studentship, 105, 111
Journal of Anatomy and Physiology, foundation of, 70, 71
Journal of Hygiene, foundation of, 118
Journal of Pathology and Bacteriology, foundation of, 115
Journal of Physiology, foundation of, 71, 82, 90

Kanthack Memorial Libraries, 112
King (Nita) Research Scholarship, 106

Laboratory accommodation, 30
Levy Fund and Studentship in Biochemistry, 99
Lewes (George Henry) Studentship in Physiology, 84
Licence to practise physic, 4; discontinued, 22; improved examination for, 20, 21; number conferred, 11, 21, 22; qualification of candidates for, 23
Licence to practise surgery, 2, 4, 5; discontinuance of, 22
Licensed Teachers of Anatomy, 52
Linacre Lectureship, endowment of, 6, 7; foundation of, 6, 213; honorarium of Lecturer, 219; Lecturers, 213–220; qualifications of Lecturer, 7; subjects of the Lecture, 7, 219
London, early practice of physic in, 5, 159
London School of Tropical Medicine and Hygiene, 43

London University, 23

Marmaduke Sheild Scholarship, 55
Materia medica and therapeutics, 200, 211
Mathematical Tripos, origin of, 128
Mathematics, medicine subservient to, in seventeenth and eighteenth centuries, 8
Medical diplomas, 43; *see also* Degree
Medical education, clinical examinations, inception of, 176; clinical study, 21, 27, 104; early, 2, 4, 8, 9, 10; early English endowments for, 213; early text-books, 3, 4, 9; Edward VI's commission on, 8; enlarged curriculum, 35; expansion and improvement in, 30, 179; in eighteenth century, 14, 15, 17; in nineteenth and twentieth centuries, 20; inactivity regarding, 7, 8, 14, 15, 17; influence of the College of Physicians on, 7; influence of Padua on, 2, 8; laboratory accommodation for, 30; Natural Sciences Tripos in relation to, 23, 24, 34, 35; period of study, 29, 38; private coaching, 32; reforms and advances in, 16, 20; special diplomas, 43; suggested introduction of scholarships, 22; *see also* Degree
Medical graduates, number during the period 1500–1856, 24
Medical Jurisprudence, Lectureship in, established, 27
Medical Radiology and Electrology, Diploma in, 44
Medical scholarships, 22
Medical students, and the Natural Sciences Tripos, 35, *see also* Natural Sciences Tripos; increase in number of, 28; number in residence, 31, 34; period of study, 31
Medical Studies, Board of, 23
Medicine, Downing Chair of, 199; increase of students in, 28; Lectureships in, established and abolished, 26, 27; *see also* Degree, Physic
Michael Foster Studentship in Physiology, 83
Midwifery, Lectureship in, 26, 27

Molteno Institute for Research in Parasitology, 33, 118
Moral Sciences Tripos, establishment of, 21
Muscular physiology, 153

Natural Experimental Philosophy, establishment of chair of, 17
Natural Science Club, 25
Natural sciences, cultivation of, 178
Natural Sciences Tripos, and the medical curriculum, 10, 23, 24, 26, 35, 37, 69; establishment of, 21, 50, 179; number of entries for (1887 and 1921), 34; women admitted to, 21
Nita King Research Scholarship, 106

Ordinances, 45, 46
Ordo Senioritatis, 128, 190
Oxford University, clinical instruction at, 30; early medical teaching at, 3; Linacre Lectureships at, 6; "Philosophicall Clubbe" at, 9, 10; Regius Professors at, 120; Royal College of Physicians and graduates of, 5, 7, 10, 19, 29, 159, 160; Royal Commission (1919), 33; teaching of anatomy at, 53, 54

Padua, influence of, on medical education, 2, 8, 191
Papworth Village Settlement, 115, 188
Parasitology, foundation of, 118
Parasitology, Molteno Institute for Research in, 33, 118
Pathological Society of Great Britain and Ireland, foundation of, 115
Pathology, biology in relation to, 104; growth of the study of, 88; importance of, 69, 102; Lectureships, Demonstratorships and Studentships in, 105; Professors of, 107–116
Pathology, Department of, 102–106; growth and work of, 102–105; Professorship established, 26, 102, 109; stipend of the Professors, 105
Perse School, 132

Pharmacology, Lectureship and Reader in, 200
Pharmacology and therapeutics, 211
"Philosophicall Clubbe", at Oxford, 9, 10
Physic, early practice of, in London, 3, 5, 150, 159, 160; early text-books of, 3–4; Licence to practise, 4, 5; Linacre Lectureship in, 213–216; "Scoles of Fisyk", 3
Physic, Regius Professorship of, 120–126
Physic, Regius Professors of, and Addenbrooke's Hospital, 30, 165, 185; characteristics of, 124; early duties of, 11; grant of arms to, 125, 136; inactivity of, 11, 14, 15, 17, 18; stipend of, 120, 123, 124
Physiological Laboratory, establishment of, 17; opening of, 33
Physiological Society, 82; foundation of, 71, 90
Physiologists, famous, 81, 82, 86, 91
Physiology, 87 89; chair of, established, 26, 70, 81, 88; chemical, 98, *see also* Biochemistry; Department of, 79–84; early students of, 84; early teaching of, 79; growth of the study of, 87; microscopical anatomy in the teaching of, 77; Praelector in, 79, 80, 83, 87; Professors of, 85–97; Readerships, Lectureships and Demonstrators in, 26, 83, 91; Studentships and Prizes in, 83
Physwick's Hostel, 190
Pinsent-Darwin Fund and Studentship, 101
Plague visitation (1629–1630), 145
Plant physiology, 81
Post-graduate Research Hospital, need for, 27
Pretty (Gwynaeth) Research Fund and Studentship, 105
Preventive Medicine, Readership in, 105
Prize fellowships, 34
Private coaching, 31, 32
Psychological Medicine, Diploma in, 43

234

Psychology, experimental, 82, 100; Department of, 100–101; growth of the study of, 100
Psychopathology, Lectureship in, 101
Public Health, Diploma in, 43, 179

Quick Chair of Biology, 117–118

Radcliffe Infirmary, foundation of, 162
Radiology, Diploma in, 44
Ray Club, 178
Raymond Horton-Smith Prize, 41
Rede Lecturers, 72, 88
Regius Professors, 7, 120; inactivity of, in eighteenth century, 14, 15, 17, 18; *see also* Physic, Regius Professor of
"Resurrectionists", 51, 59, 61
Rickets, earliest treatises on, 153, 154
Rockefeller Foundation, 81, 103
Rolleston Memorial Prize, 83
Royal College of Physicians, 5, 7, 149, 159, 160; and the practice of physic in London, 5; early actions against, 5, 159; early privileges of, 5, 159; foundation of, 5; influence on medical education, 7; insignia of, 196; Oxford and Cambridge graduates in relation to, 5, 10, 19, 159, 160; suggested granting of medical degrees by, 29, 170
Royal College of Surgeons, M.R.C.S. Diploma, 25; suggested granting of degrees by, 29
Royal Colleges of Physicians and Surgeons, special diplomas granted by, 43
Royal Commission (of 1548), 8; (of 1850), 21, 46; (of 1877), 46; (of 1919), 33, 46
Royal mandate degrees, 12
Royal Society, 152; foundation of, 9

Scholarships, medical, 22
Scientific research, early, 9
"Senior Wrangler maker", 32
Sheild (Marmaduke) Scholarship, 55
Sir William Dunn Biochemical Department, 33, 98
Statutes, 2, 15, 45, 46, 135; Elizabethan, 10, 15, 46, 135, 136; *Statuta antiqua*, 10, 15, 45, 46
Studies from the Physiological Laboratory in the University of Cambridge, 82
Surgery, 69; chair of, established, 26, 221; Licence to practise, 2, 4, 5, 22; Readership, Lectureship and Demonstratorship in, 26, 27, 223; *see also* Degree
Sweating sickness, 153, 192, 213

Tancred Studentships, 22
Thermometer, clinical, introduction of, 182
Theses, 23; for the M.B. degree, 39; for the M.D. degree, 40, 41; importance of, 40
Tripos, see Natural Sciences Tripos; Medical, 69
Tropical Medicine and Hygiene, Diploma in, 43, 186
Tuberculosis, Papworth Village Settlement for, 115, 188

Walker (John Lucas) Studentship and Exhibitions, 105; holders of, 111
Waynflete Professor of Physiology, 87
Women, 186; admission to M.B. and M.D. examinations, 21, 42; forbidden to practise physic, 3; number in residence (1929–1930), 34
Wranglers and private coaching, 32

Zoology, chair of, established, 53, 64

CAMBRIDGE : PRINTED BY
W. LEWIS, M.A.
AT THE UNIVERSITY PRESS